Resources of Christianity

Resources of Christianity

François Jullien

Translated by Pedro Rodriguez

polity

Originally published in French as *Ressources du christianisme.* © Éditions de L'Herne, 2018. Published by arrangement with Agence littéraire Astier-Pécher. ALL RIGHTS RESERVED

This English edition © 2021 by Polity Press

Polity Press
65 Bridge Street
Cambridge CB2 1UR, UK

Polity Press
101 Station Landing
Suite 300
Medford, MA 02155, USA

ISBN-13: 978-1-5095-4695-4- hardback
ISBN-13: 978-1-5095-4696-1- paperback

A catalogue record for this book is available from the British Library.

Library of Congress Cataloging-in-Publication Data

Names: Jullien, François, 1951- author. | Rodríguez, Pedro, 1933- translator.
Title: Resources of Christianity / François Jullien ; translated by Pedro Rodriguez.
Other titles: Ressources du christianisme. English
Description: Cambridge, UK ; Medford. MA, USA : Polity Press, [2021] | Originally published in French as Ressources du christianisme. Editions de L'Herne, 2018. | Includes bibliographical references. | Summary: "A fresh and erudite reflection on Christianity and its relevance today"-- Provided by publisher.
Identifiers: LCCN 2020041424 (print) | LCCN 2020041425 (ebook) | ISBN 9781509546954 (hardback) | ISBN 9781509546961 (paperback) | ISBN 9781509546978 (epub) | ISBN 9781509547043 (pdf)
Subjects: LCSH: Christianity--Philosophy. | Bible. John--Criticism, interpretation, etc.
Classification: LCC BR100 .J8513 2021 (print) | LCC BR100 (ebook) | DDC 230--dc23
LC record available at https://lccn.loc.gov/2020041424
LC ebook record available at https://lccn.loc.gov/2020041425

Typeset in 12.5 on 15 pt Adobe Garamond by
Servis Filmsetting Ltd, Stockport, Cheshire
Printed and bound by Short Run Press Limited

For further information on Polity, visit our website:
politybooks.com

For Pascal David

This text expands on a lecture I gave in March 2016 for the *Cours méthodique et populaire de philosophie* at the Bibliothèque Nationale de France, and in May 2016 at the Université Catholique de Lyon.

My thanks to Pascal David, who edited the first written version.

Contents

I

Refusal to avoid (the question of Christianity)

Why, you might wonder, have I decided to deal today with "Christianity"? What more have we to do with it? I believe it's important at present to take the trouble, to stop evading the question, because it is a fertile one: not for cultural identity (is Europe "Christian"?) but for culture, and especially for philosophy, which is the matter at hand. The eras of Christianity's dominance and subsequent denunciation are behind us, and the era of its banishment upon us. It is high time to review what Christianity has caused to advene[1] in thought. What *possibilities* of the mind has it contributed, or buried? That is my reason. Because it needs doing. Even if, having spent so much time among the Greeks and the Chinese, I am perhaps not ideally suited to the task. Perhaps the risk is worthwhile for me precisely because I take an external perspective, because I am further removed from the vassal's position.

I believe the time has come to stop evading the question of Christianity in contemporary thought. The very idea of "Europe," bound up as it is in that history, stands to gain. We in present-day Europe must determine what Christianity has contributed, transformed, discovered, or covered up in thought. We must determine what lies totalized (labeled) in the *-ity* of Christianity, which we see couched amid so many other *-ities* and *-isms*. I say *evading* [*évitement*] because the astonishing, even aberrant, affair known as Christianity is, in an ambient manner, a collective embarrassment to us. There is no denying this. We would like to see it over and done with, filed away. We would like to believe it to be a historical matter. And so we tacitly skirt the issue. But can we be rid of it? From Lacan to Mitterrand, a Mass is, *in fine*, perhaps not out of the question. . . . Even as we bother with so many false questions – questions that no longer deserve the name, questions that we keep alive in artificial debates – we shut our eyes to the matter of genuine import in this troubling heritage of ours. Officially declaring our society to be secular has hardly unburdened us of Christianity, that "thing" we now find so difficult to grasp. Though a massive majority of us no longer "believes" – or, at any rate, no longer "practices" (there are so many passive Christians) – we have hardly obliterated Christianity's imprint from our thought. We know this, of course, but how deeply do we *wish to know it?* Even if all that remained were a relic, we would still have to wonder what part of Christianity we could not get past. I wonder, in fact, if this evasion doesn't extend into the Church itself, more comfortable now with ecology and humanitarianism than with the question I do not see being asked: What has Christianity *done to thought?*

Needless to say, I will not enter into the matter of Christianity with the traditional question: to "believe" or not. "He who believed in heaven / He who did not"[2] seems to me a somewhat outmoded dilemma. I will not first delve into Christianity from the standpoint of "faith." Even the question whether "God" exists seems to me to have run its course. Though still of interest for the history of thought, it has bogged down completely. Perhaps it will recover some of its relevance later on, in some other configuration of the mind, but for present-day thought it is a dead issue, with no further effect. Christian philosophers themselves, drawing a lesson from Kant, have shown that all imaginable proofs for the existence of God lead nowhere. Christianity has no use for the crutch of demonstration. That said, neither will I seek refuge in the history of thought, a field in which I have no competence. Nor, more generally, will I consider Christianity from the scholarly, remote, disinterested perspective of the social sciences. Such exteriority no longer stands in relation to its cultural tradition. It stems from an adopted "objective" position, and would necessarily quash whatever existential gain I might draw from Christianity's thought. To explore such potential gain we must *enter into* Christianity's thought – but does "entering into" mean *adherence*? How, then, can we develop a philosophy that is no longer Christian per se – as honorable as such philosophy is, thanks to many great names (Augustine, Pascal, Kierkegaard, and, today in France, Jean-Luc Marion, Jean-Louis Chrétien, and Michel Henry) – but is instead a *philosophy of Christianity*? A philosophy

4

whose perspective is not the traditional one of apologetics and criticism, defense and denunciation? After all, we have before us a question that does not run through the rift and concerns us all equally: do the coherences of Christianity, the mostly paradoxical coherences, still have a use in thought, especially in the thought of *existence*? In other words, how might they remain pertinent if, in fact, we are no longer required to believe?

A quick doubling-back to warn of paths that I will not follow. There are at least three, forming a triangle. First off, to undertake a philosophy of Christianity is not to subject it to philosophical reason, or to bend it to reason's criteria. Nor is it to reduce Christianity to the most reasonable, or most acceptable, moral content. This would reduce Scripture to the most elementary of teachings, for purely practical use. Christianity's sole article of faith would then be "obeisance out of love for thy neighbor," its sole credo that "there exists a supreme being that loves justice and charity" (Spinoza's *Theological-Political Treatise*). It is one thing to take faith and *boil it down* to its supposed minimal content, like Spinoza, and thereby forsake what might be the most singular and inventive aspects of Christian teaching. It is another to enter into Christian thinking, as I am proposing to do, *without first passing through faith*, and by the same token without losing – in the manner of a minimalist (rationalist) reduction – what are potentially the most daring, and therefore most fertile, aspects of its conception. It is true that Spinoza, even as he undertook his rationalization, thought it necessary to conduct a rigorous, linguistically and historically buttressed, exegesis, so as to judge the texts' authority critically, with a focus on "meaning" instead of "truth." Already with Spinoza, then, we have a promising start. He opened the way to jettisoning the traditional, preliminary criterion of belief.

At the same time, a philosophy of Christianity needn't run counter to Spinozism, serving as its flipside, and give up the cause of reason. It needn't illustrate Christianity by invoking the poetry or the bigger soul[3] it has brought to the human experience (like Chateaubriand in *The Genius of Christianity*). The "soul" would never be content with an explanation, which will always come up short. It would cry out for "mystery": "The most marvelous sentiments are those that stir a certain confusion in us." This facile binary, in which the "vagueness" of the religious offsets the rigor of science, is suspect by its very convenience. The peal of evening bells in the countryside (or the Latin chants of the Church, or the paintings of Fra Angelico, etc.) might indeed convey emotion, but before drawing an argument from this we must declare what makes it religiously specific. The Christian religion, says Chateaubriand, has tended the "secret," developed a "sense of the sacred," but couldn't we say the same of many other religions? And, in praising Christianity by comparison, we would fall, as Chateaubriand inevitably falls, into the trap of ethnocentrism. As we now know, the way of comparison with other religions leads nowhere. It rests entirely on ignorance of other cultures or, worse, on contempt for the Other, who serves only as the negative of his own affirmation. "The Romans," says Chateaubriand, "were a horrible people." This eulogy *a contrario* holds up only inasmuch as we *enter into* one coherence rather than the other – the comparison is justified only from within the extolled religion. Chateaubriand, partaking of the nascent Romanticism, did indeed begin to develop the concept of *modernity*. He also brought out the *subjectivity* that was effectively being promoted in Christianity. But what religion anywhere in the world lacks its own "genius"?

The inverse path, doubling back to Spinozism, albeit from a different angle, is the path of *demystification*. Here, rather than extoll Christianity, we must denounce Christianity's "mystery." We must reveal its illusion, and to do that we must reduce it to its "essence" (Feuerbach's *The Essence of Christianity*). Spilling over the "national" framework and ethnic limits of the God of Israel, the nature of Christianity, says Feuerbach, has been to raise human aspiration, perceived in its universality, to the heights of the absolute. In other words, Feuerbach established the primacy of the subjective (sentiment: *das Gemüt*) over objectivity (as determined by science), to the point of reducing the one to the other. In still other words, he took the satisfaction of subjective (affective) needs and objectified them in God. This betokens the triumph of "love" over the "law" – whether nature's or society's. God is he who "says yes" to my wishes, impossible as they might be. This is why in Feuerbach's eyes Christian faith amounts to belief in miracles. God can grant my aspiration, even if it contravenes the necessity of nature (death). In Christianity desire is elevated [*exhaussé*], as well as fulfilled [*exaucé*], until it transmutes into the most intimate certainty – becoming unconditional – of awareness [*conscience*]. *Even if* the fulfillment contradicts our understanding, or the facts of experience, and brings us up against the "unthinkable" (*undenkbar*). The fulfillment occurs instantly, meeting with no resistance from the world and requiring no patient effort of knowledge, for a miracle is "as rapid as a wish is impatient,"[4] but what could it be if not a fiction where we mistake our desires for reality? What could it be if not the production and projection of an imagination that dreams as it likes of happiness, and never works towards it?

Freud takes things no further (in *The Future of an Illusion*). All our "anti-theology" textbooks rehash the same arguments. But can we leave it at that? What has Feuerbach's analysis, though apt and even elucidating, been compelled to overlook? What has its initial choice forced it unwittingly to leave aside? Christianity might indeed have promoted subjectivity, but it remains to be seen whether we should understand its particular notion of the "subjective" as the correlate of the objective in science's determination. It remains to be seen whether we have, on principle, come to misapprehend subjectivity inasmuch as Christianity has revealed it *not to respond to objectivity*, inasmuch as Christianity has, in advance, left their pairing in suspense and, as it were, imperfect. If we set the miracle, the prodigy that contravenes reason (water changed to wine at Cana), at the core of Christian faith, then what are we to make of the fact that such a prodigy is referred to explicitly not as a "miracle" (*Wunder*) but as a "sign" (*sēmeîon*, σημεῖον, in Greek)? It is others who demand prodigy-miracles (*terata*, τέρατα); Christ, for his part, produces signs (cf. John 4:48).[5] Doesn't the substitution of *sign* for *miracle* produce an immediate shift in thought, directing it towards something else (other than thaumaturgy)? Moreover, in viewing it strictly from the perspective of non-contradiction, like Feuerbach, do we not immediately close reason off from paradox, the very thing to which Christianity has so powerfully contributed, the very thing whose intelligence Christianity has deployed? Indeed, can the positing of God as the objectification of desire obscure what Christianity, following in Judaism's wake, invites us to discover, under the figure of God, as the *encounter with the Other*? Though a bit too quick to dispense with the question of the "world" – of its consistency, and thus also of its resistance to desire – Christian thought on the matter of subjectivity has an essential link with alterity, which itself compels an effective spilling-over from the world [*fait effectivement déborder du monde*].

That Christianity might be an entirely human production does not account for the entirety of its import. That its content might in fact be "anthropological," as Feuerbach says, should not lead us to overlook what it has promoted and invented in man. For the term *essence* in *The Essence of Christianity* rightly has another use. Not only does it speak to the specificity of Christianity, it more importantly, more radically, serves to define the religion as "the relation of man to his own nature [i.e., essence][6]." Therein lies its truth. But Christianity, adds Feuerbach, recognizes man's essence not as his own but as that of another, extant in itself ("God"), separate from man, and even standing in opposition to him. And therein lies its falsity. In this respect religion is, as Marx would say, "alienating." But in rendering this judgment – that is, in bringing the "celestial" down to the earth of anthropology – must we necessarily restrict man's "essence" to a particular fixed content, to a fixable content? Must we thereby forget that "man" is a creature in mid-becoming – or, better yet, mid-advent? For man is ceaselessly detaching from himself, precisely to *make himself other*. Therein lies his capacity to *abide outside of himself* [*se tenir hors de soi*] and properly "ex-ist." Even from a strictly human perspective, hasn't Christianity opened new possibilities unto man (opened them *in* man)? We cannot be content, like Feuerbach, with an *explanation* of Christianity as a phenomenon, as every explanation is reductive, and we will risk failing to see the *exploratory* and effectively productive aspects within Christianity. Baldly stated, my question here is as follows: is Christianity's productive capacity – what lays within its power to *develop within man* – now exhausted?

I will steer clear, then, of these three well-trodden paths, all leading through the sole plain of belief. I will guard against bringing Christianity into the sphere of reason, which will seek to steer it towards a more generally acceptable ethical good sense – though this once had the merit of drawing Europe out of dogmatic and bloody conflicts. I will also not do the reverse and set Christianity against reason, finding justification in its aura of mystery – though this once served to emancipate subjectivity, primarily from the sclerotic rationality to which the Enlightenment had led. Finally, I will not be content to *explain* Christianity, and fail in my analysis of its "essence" to grasp what it might promote in terms of *existence* – though this too, historically, was once necessary, so that, within its exigency, the possibility of science could assert itself separately from religion. The genealogy I would point to here, if we need one, goes back through Nietzsche, paradoxically enough. Nietzsche wondered what Christianity had both perverted and refined in "man" as he had *become* in Europe. What had this cost in terms of Greek heroism and happiness? Moreover, what manner of abyssal interiority, what *possible* subjectivity, had it subsequently carved out, even in its culture of resentment towards life? Nietzsche, however, dealt in terms of "values," counseled and even foretold against Christianity a "transvaluation of values," *Umwertung aller Werte*, because values are indeed exclusive. But must we end things there, at exclusion? For this reason I will deal in terms not of "values" but of *resources*.

II

Resources

The nature of a resource – to return to a concept that has become central to my work – is to be *explored* and *exploited*, and to be explored further in its exploitation. In a resource the bipartition between knowledge on the one side and action on the other, between theory and practice, breaks down. A resource is, as such, nobody's property; it does not *belong* (this is why I reject the notion of cultural identity). A resource goes to whoever discovers it – the more deeply he discovers it – and draws benefit from it. Because it retains a measure of potential, because it counts on a future in which to deploy, a resource is not something to delimit or define from the start. We do not instantly know its nature or limits. A resource exists only insofar as we have developed it. It therefore entails responsibility. We activate a resource or do not. We might just as easily over-look it, or else see it and pass it by. Christianity, then, offers "resources" inasmuch as there are gains to be had from it – inasmuch as it can give rise to effects, without previous determination as to its truth. After all, hasn't Truth – with its disjunctive structure (true or false), which both theology and philosophy are dead set on – ended up sterilizing thought? Has it not impoverished thought's resource? Or is it perhaps better to take "truth" to be a resource of thought – a major resource, but one of many?

This is why I will be dealing here with the *resources* of Christianity, rather than asking first about Christianity's dogmatic truth. I will be taking an exploratory approach, then, prospect-ing for seams by poking about. Resources of Christianity, and not *the* resources of Christianity. No limiting definite article. As when I explore the resources of Greek or Chinese thought. For I always begin with the same, elementary ques-tion: what benefit (profit) to draw? I will read the Gospels as I would read any other text – that is, by trying to answer the same question: what lies behind the text's *coherence* (rather than its "meaning," already too selective and directed a notion)? What accounts for its pertinence – where *pertinence* avoids the trap of what has been sealed up as truth. And, as I have said, all without any need to *adhere*. The exploitation of resources demands no conversion. I have not "gone Taoist" over the years. Thus the traditional opposition between the sacred and the profane is lifted. The status accorded to the text, whether it is "religious" or not, matters little from the global perspective of a resource. Also lifted is the opposition between thought and life. "Resources" applies alike to thought and to life: resources of thought, resources of life. "Now I think, now I live," says the adage, tragically forging an alternative. The notion of a *resource* undoes this discord as well.

We will come to understand resources better by examining what they are not. First off, a *resource* is not a *value*. "Value" has exploded the traditional notion of Good in contemporary thought, undermining its onto-theological foundations: its absolute, or at least socially imposed, "in-itself-ness." Values, as Nietzsche teaches, are "perspectives," and therefore depend on the evaluation and judgment that we each rightfully bring to bear. Thus any unitary (safeguarding) and normative character is undone, as perspectives are necessarily plural – and, indeed, mutually exclusive: one cannot exist at the same time as another. Values are rivals, too. They contest one another and compete. They are thus extolled and even preached. And they are consequently liable to turn gregarious and slide into intolerance. We desperately want them to serve a collective identity, and are quick to raise our voices and become intransigent in defending "our" values. For an example we need only look to Nietzsche himself. Christian values are just as subject to this condition as other values. What's more, in the present-day world they seem even more dubious, or at least more hotly debated. Such are the values of "purity," "submission," "humility," and all exaltations of woe, not to mention the infantilism that Nietzsche denounced. – Fortunately, however, "resources" are not "values." Resources do not compete. They compound as we branch out in their exploration, and they enrich one another by their divides [*écarts*]. They do not excommunicate one another. I can draw from the resources of Christian thought as I can from those of Taoist thought, and the former reflect off the latter. Thus we needn't extoll or preach resources. They are on offer to whosoever can deploy them.

"Resources," moreover, are not "riches." Yet would we not speak readily of the "spiritual riches" of the Gospels as so many precious goods to be maintained and enriched? But such riches lull us to sleep. At best we see to their transmission. Indeed, their transmission has become a major concern in this day and age, now that our ways of life and ideas demand ever-faster renewal if we hope to keep up with our technical revolutions, and now that education can no longer expect its content to remain changeless. The notion of *resource* stands in direct opposition to the neglect of such riches, a neglect we deplore as we recall the mind to its duty. Whereas riches readily claim to be perennial and of certain value, resources lead us to consider them valuable only insofar as each of us, each generation, makes an effort to activate them, from scratch, so as both to explore and to exploit them. Resources exist only insofar as we make them bear fruit. At the same time, the potential that lies within keeps them soaring [*en essor*] and frees them from the limits to which the present moment is subject in its slackness [*étalement*].[1] Potential extracts them from the miring positivity of the finished and the accepted. We do not know the limits of the resources we explore, whereas the riches we possess are walled in from the start. In this regard the notion of the *resource* is salutary for Christianity. It renders service by dethroning Christianity from the self-arrogated preeminence it enjoyed while it was the dominant ideology, and in which it wilted. It thus forces Christianity to get back to work, if it hopes to survive, and to rethink itself: to take on some risk once more. Lest its resource die.

In other words, *resource* is not *root* and should in fact be considered as contrary. "Root" knocks the cultural (spiritual) down to the level of the natural. Worse, it worships at the altar of the mythic unitary-primordial: the myth of a first Beginning. The "Christian roots of France"? The baptism of Clovis. But what did "baptism" mean at the time to Clovis? And what, then, are we to make of "our ancestors the Gauls"? Or of the "Christian roots of Europe" – as if Europe hadn't found just as many resources in the promotion of rationality as a bulwark against faith. Yet we in no way mean here to deny the importance of

Christianity in France or in European history; or the historically local mark that Christianity bears within itself; or the measure of tradition that every religion necessarily turns into its capital. We mean only to reject the inherited belonging and dependence that "root" presupposes. *Root* looks backwards, and therefore buries. *Resource* is productive, because it prospects. Moreover, *root* entails identity, and thus sectarianism, whereas *resource* is a call to share. In fact, it has been the nature of Christianity to un-root [*dé-raciner*] – or, better yet, uproot [*désenraciner*] – Judaism: to detach it from its ethnic markers. "Root" thus runs precisely counter to what seems to be one of Christianity's chief resources: the requirement of universality. "Neither Greek nor Jew," "neither man nor woman," "neither master nor slave": by neutralizing all differences – cultural, sexual, social – Paul brings the Greek ideal of abstract universalities (concepts) down to humanity's concrete condition – or at least makes the ideal into a principle. "Root" openly contradicts this.

This is also why it is perhaps not so warranted to begin our inquiry by positing the "truth" of Christianity, or making faith the condition of entry. Such entry would necessarily split us into two camps: "believers"/"non-believers." A resource, however, is by nature available – that is, available to all, open to all, and knows no border. We explore a resource insofar as we see a "resource" in it. But "faith" is trenchant. It must produce a rupture (the "leap"), and thus proceeds from an arbitrary beginning. By isolating itself and setting itself up as a preliminary, faith always runs the risk of arising subjectively from some form of autosuggestion (I believe because I want to believe) and objectively from sedimentation and ossification (leading to dogma). Furthermore, Christianity seems to me clumsiest – or, let us say, most lacking in resources – precisely when it seeks to convince us of its truth. We need only consider Paul, purportedly its great preacher, to see the inanity of some of Christianity's arguments. Witness the old Stoic argument, as imperishable as it is useless:[2] God is evident in his works, which are the world's beauty. Or the bargain (later the wager): let us accept "our light affliction"[3] for an eternity of glory. Or intimidation (hell) and accusation (if you do not believe, you must be bad). Or else the forced alternative clamping down like a vise: if we do not believe in the resurrection, we are simply to "drink and eat" without constraint, "for tomorrow we die."[4] Christianity might contain other resources than these paltry offerings.

But the idea here is not to abolish the specificity – and thus capacity – of a resource as we liberate it from trenchant faith. Just as it sets no "borders," no confines in which to exhaust itself, a resource is always singular, and takes pride in its originality and invention. A resource does not leave us hanging on the disjunctive function of truth, but neither does it let us lapse into flat ecumenism (the supper in *Zadig*). Though not insensible to the collective gesture of good will, I wonder what it could possibly mean to see, as one does nowadays, a priest, a rabbi, a pastor, an imam, and even, more recently, a Buddhist monk co-officiating a national ceremony of mourning. Might these various, so-called religious expressions be just so many paths – so many modes of address – to the same "God"? For me "God" is interesting to ponder only when there's daring in the thinking, and this demands singularity. Are we still thinking in terms of "God" if we shift away from "monotheism"? The common denominator between these religious manifestations is necessarily small, for where is this postulated point at which all religions meet? "Spirituality," the consensual term now in fashion, is insufficient. More to the point, the "spiritual" is a false universal. As well intentioned as it is, I cannot but wonder whether the act of solidarity doesn't entail, under cover of tolerance and just representation, a loss of resources in *every one* of those religious traditions. Is it not a way to unload a responsibility that we can no longer shoulder: in short, an alibi? Resources do not exclude one another, but neither do they brook conflation. They are amenable to sharing but not to trivialization. Like all other propositions of thought, religious propositions are to be no more diluted than imposed, lest their content, and thus what constitutes their resource, run dry.

In casting about for a resource that, because effectively liminal, could serve as an entry into Christianity – an entry that is not divisive, like the statement of truth, but detonating – we might settle first on the singular fact that the Gospels are written in Greek, even though Christ knew no Greek and spoke Aramaic. Thus Christ's message is delivered in a different language – indeed, a language of different provenance (Indo-European and not Semitic) – from the one spoken by

Christ himself. And not just any language. It is Greek, the language that gave us the concept and promoted philosophy. Christian teaching finds itself peeled away from its idiom, detached from its linguistic heritage, removed from its implications, and thereby drawn into the requirement of universality that it turned into its message. But let us return to the concepts of the *divide* [*écart*] and *interspace* [*l'entre*], which figure prominently in my work, upstream even from the concept of *resource*. It seems to me that Christianity has gained from the divide between languages in which it has historically been situated, and that this *inter-language interspace* has contributed to its fertility. Rather than sink into – recline on[5] – such self-evidence as a single medium would secrete, the text of the Gospels is worked by [*travaillé par*] translation from one language to another. Or else the evangelist sets the languages side by side, in *juxta*: "They said unto him, 'Rabbi' (which is to say, being interpreted, 'Master' [*didaskalos*, διδάσκαλος])."[6] The two terms, stemming from two such diverging cultural traditions, reflect in each other, each going beyond its limit through the other. (We might also consider *Messiah* and *Christos* (Χριστός).) Even the final inscription on the cross, the ultimate message, is, as John notes, in Hebrew, Latin, and Greek. From this *divide* between languages Christianity has promoted a *common* [*un commun*] of thought that, in crossing cultural diversity, is an intensive common.

The *divide* sets tension while at the same time bringing out *interspace*, because it opens up a distance. And through this distance occurs the translation of a common that is not impoverished, like the common of resemblance, but intensive. This is without a doubt one of the Gospels' first fertile teachings. It is not declared, in the manner of a truth, but *implemented* [*mise en œuvre*]. It is a function of its very mechanism, which sets up a second, structural divide, other than that between languages. Because there is not one Gospel but four, facing off and juxtaposed. Unlike *difference*, which leaves aside the other once a distinction is established, a *divide* maintains the face-off, and thus the tension, between what it has separated. It keeps the separated things staring at each other [*maintient le dévisagement*].[7] What occurs in the Gospels is not a nesting of [*mise en abîme*] but a divide between accounts [*mise en écart*], and this divide is productive because, in and of itself, it continually calls upon the four Gospels, from the active *interspace* between them, to question one another and go beyond themselves. The Gospels are not just various versions that only corroborate one another, saying more or less the same thing, or that we should bring together in an attempt at synthesis. They are four paths each venturing forth in its own way onto that perilous terrain where we utter the possibility of the impossible. They provide no glimpse of a happy medium between them. Rather, they lay out a diversity of perspectives that spill over one another, while also questioning and elucidating one another reciprocally in their respective singularity. There will thus be no single, canonical account but four parallel attempts to lend credence to the unheard-of [*l'inoui*]. We can try to deal with the ever-so-cumbersome affair of the one we call "Christ" by moralizing, like Matthew, or psychologizing, like Mark, or mythologizing, like Luke (a gross oversimplification, I admit). John, for his part, radicalizes. All in light of a single question: what is it to be effectively alive? In this I will follow John.

III

An event is possible

A divide [*écart*] away from Paul and the other evangelists, John makes no mention of the novelty signaled or attested to by Christianity. But he is keen to think through the very possibility of an *event* that is, as such, necessarily unheard-of [*inouï*], and to demonstrate that life *is* this pure *eventuality*.[1] He does not remind us, like Mark, that we mustn't sew a new piece of cloth onto an old garment or pour new wine into old bottles. He does not urge us, like Paul, to strip the "old man" to clothe the new. Indeed, to deal with "newness" we must take a step back from our representations, set up a comparison, and pass judgment; we must take a bird's-eye view of the history in question. Affirming the new implies an ideological procedure that urges rupture. Such is the nature of Paul's teaching: the "first" and the "last" Adam.[2] John, however, eschews ideology, or minimizes it. He is keen to examine the possibility of an event within Christianity, with respect not to a historical Break (before/after) but to the event's very arising. Hence John's chief concern is to set the event within Being and, for this reason, to connect the becoming of the eventual[3] with the timeless or the eternal. The Greeks had given becoming careful thought, but saw it always as a diminution of being, always as inextricably linked with generation and corruption, and therefore as lacking any consistency of its own. Thus for the Greeks being alone "is" effectively ("really [*étantement*]" (*ontôs*, όντως), says Plato). Herein lies John's revolution. John recasts the capacity for becoming as an event.

This, then, is where John begins, in his prologue, or his entryway into Christianity. Right away he establishes *becoming* – which is not only the event's locus but also its condition of possibility – in relation to *being*. While certainly still dependent on being, becoming is no longer opposed to being, and thus no longer disdained. Our two terms, *becoming* and *being*, are linked:

the one is established on the basis of the other, but no longer set beneath it or in its shadow. "Was [*était*]" and "became [*devint*]" occur in succession (imperfect to aorist: *en/egéneto*): "In the beginning was the Word, and the Word was with God. . . ." Then (a *then* of pure enunciation, with no further transition): "All things became through him, and without him nothing became." Because it is understood here in the absolute sense, *become* takes on a new meaning; in John's Greek *become* becomes *advene*. John begins by saying that an advent is possible. This is the strict object of his announcement. We cannot help but read that all things "became" – that is, "advened" – by him. The decisive divide opens between the inconsistent *becoming* of metaphysics and the *advent* through which events arise. It is this "became [*devint*]" (advened) that, step by step, gradually forms John's prologue and structures its opening: "There advened a man dispatched by God"; "the world advened through him"; "the Word advened as flesh"; "for the law was given by Moses, but grace and truth advened through Jesus Christ."[4]

I am therefore surprised that the (official?) translation (by the Ecole Biblique de Jérusalem) does not abide by the structuring "advened," which John uses at every point in the development, without the slightest variation, and which takes on the (unitary) value of a concept. I am surprised, in fact, that the translation should conflate the two modalities of "being" and "becoming" despite John's careful distribution of terms. Instead of the literal "all things advened by him" we get "all things were by him" ("and without him nothing was"). Instead of "there advened a man" (sent by God) we get "there appeared a man." Instead of "the logos [the Word][5] advened as flesh," we get "and the Word was made flesh." Instead of "grace and truth advened through Jesus Christ," we get "grace and truth came to us by Jesus Christ." *From the very start*, then, John's announcement – that the foundation of what we will call Christianity is the consideration of an event's very possibility – is muddled. It is muddled before we are ever asked to believe that a particular event (Christ's resurrection) is possible. Thus John begins upstream from the matter of faith; he begins with the question of what we must think if we are to consider the event in terms of its condition. "All things were by him," because it dissolves becoming in being, instantly leaves no room in thought for an event. "There appeared a man" reduces the event by presenting it from the (external) perspective of a spectator. "The Word was made flesh" adds *made*, and thus artifice, which raises the question of modality, and even of intention. "Grace and truth came to us by Jesus Christ" shifts us away from becoming and towards "coming," which we must now locate and attribute in order to justify. In every instance we lose the strict nudity of the event (of the single *egéneto*, ἐγένετο), even as consistency should be gradually building from one occurrence to the next. Yet it is the nudity of the event that John rigorously speaks of, and that we should read literally.

Let no one reply that these are just manners of speaking (of translating), for such manners of speaking (of translating) are always also manners of thinking; and John's *became* (*advened*) is effectively matrical.[6] It punctuates John's entire text, and thus constitutes the eventual at its most elementary stage. Not "And the third day there was a marriage in Cana of Galilee" (as the ordinary translation[7] reads) but "there advened [*egéneto*] a marriage in Cana."[8] Not "These sayings caused a division once more among the Jews," but "A division once more advened among the Jews."[9] This is important for the intelligibility in John's Gospel of what we traditionally call a "miracle": what reason seeks to naturalize by force (Spinoza) or else denounce as a fiction, the mere objectivized projection of desire (Feuerbach). In John's Gospel Jesus says to the infirm man not "Wilt thou be made whole?" (the ordinary translation) but "Wilt thou become [advene] whole?" (*hygiès genésthai*, ὑγιὴς γενέσθαι). And then not "the man was made whole" but "the man became [advened] whole." "Be made whole [*guérir*]" in its passive form ("was made whole [*fut guéri*]") refers to the eventuality of a transitive act, that of a therapist or thaumaturge. But to "become [advene] whole," to restore one's "health," entails pure eventuality, and thereby escapes the causation inherent to the act of healing. For, as we know, there is no cause to an event. (Even in our schoolbooks, we in France have long given up ascribing "causes" to the French Revolution.) A "cause" remains external, an apposition from the outside. Any internal link escapes us (as Hume has said). But "advent" steers clear of this aporia by signifying only that becoming, in its deployment, leads to an event. Thus the prospect of an internal (re)generation substitutes for an external act of healing. Instead of the (stupid) question "Wilt thou heal?" (who would say no?), we have "Wilt thou advene whole?" "Will you," in other words, "accede within yourself to (hoist yourself to the level of) the *advent* from which all has advened, has always advened, since time immemorial (through me), the world included?" A divide seemingly minimal in formulation, but decisive.

John's choice is to think that there exists an *advent* opening unto a future that is not already contained in what precedes it – that is not already linked to what came before in a larger chain. The unprecedented is possible. Every morning can be a new morning in the world, peeling off from the night gone past. In other words, there must exist a pure eventuality, or, in still other words, an eventual absolute [*absolu de l'événement*], that as such has nothing to do with the becoming of Greek metaphysics, which, for lack of being, can be nothing but a repetition of the same, or sterile generation. Thus in his prologue, to establish that this category of advent is no illusion or fallacy, that an event can occur, or an advent advene, John calls Christ ("Logos," Λόγος) that "by" which

(He "by" whom) effective advent is made possible: "All things advened by him; and without him nothing advened." Or else "The world advened by him." Christ is he who, in being, opens the way to eventuality. In other words, John takes the *ontological* status to which the Greeks, in the name of being, condemned becoming and rendered it incapable of advent, and substitutes from the start another possible status, a *Christic* status, such as anchors becoming in being and grants it the capacity to innovate. "Christ" allows John to accomplish the capital task of setting becoming within being, rather than at being's margins, or in the wake of being's loss or decline. "Now I tell you before it come [i.e., before the event: literally, the becoming-advent, *prò toû genésthai*, πρὶν γενέσθαι], that, when it is come to pass [literally, "when it advenes"], ye may believe that I am."[10] Because it advenes through "Christ," the event allows us to head upstream to the Being called "Christ." Or, as he says to the dumbfounded Jews, "Before Abraham advened, I am."[11] There is indeed precedence and priority of the one over the other, of Being over becoming, but no longer any dualist break between the two. Hence a becoming can advene, and an event is possible.

The first resource in the Gospel of John, then, is the introduction into thought of the notion that an event can advene. The Greeks, for their part, at least after the development of metaphysics, failed to ascribe a reliable status to events. On the one hand, becoming, for lack of identity (lack of "being"), was for them but a metabolic corruption. On the other, they put great store in explanation: that is, in causal link (*aitía*). Causation brooks no events in the proper sense of the term, but only effects proceeding from causes. But I am just as open to the singularity of event-thought, as John establishes it, from the perspective of Chinese thought, where "events" are amenable neither to thought nor even to speech. For instance, whereas we might speak of the "events" of Tiananmen Square (in 1989) the Chinese will speak in terms that translate flatly as "affair" (*shi-jian*, 事件). Chinese, being processual, does not allow us to think of an event's *advent*, of an arising that is not already prefigured or under way (its *e-venit*), because in China an event is always the manifest, "sonorous" surfacing of a silent transformation whose gestation we can already make out further upstream. Yet it is worthwhile to ask whether an event can even

35

exist – an event that is not always just a result: i.e., that does not always proceed from what precedes it, that can bring about something completely unprecedented, unheard-of, and that might even change everything. Can a new day dawn? We know that in China the notion of (political) revolution is a wholesale import (from the West). For can there be a break between something other than two levels of reality, the "intelligible" and the "sensible," or "being" and "becoming," as with the Greeks? Can there be a break between a Before and an After? This suggests at least why so little of China was converted to Christianity after the missionaries arrived, though it had previously opened up to the Buddhism of India. In the thought of the great Clockwork of the world ("Heaven"), which, never deviating, is in ceaseless renewal, there is no room for an eventual irruption that has not been gradually primed.

Taking the thought of becoming-advent to an extreme, John tells us essentially two things. First, the event can change everything. We can leave behind our infirmity and "become whole." The event can give us entry into another life entirely. And through said event the impossible becomes possible. Second, we generally cannot perceive from the outside an event that is so very decisive: "there standeth one among you [Christ], whom ye know not."[12] For this reason John breaks ranks with the other evangelists and eschews any spectacular manifestation of the event. With Christ's death, "the veil of the temple was rent in twain" in the Gospels of Matthew, Mark, and Luke. But John makes no mention of this. For him the event is less spectacular than properly "unheard-of." In other words, it is such that we do not hear it, because we cannot hear it, for we can hear only what we have already heard. To those who ask "How opened he thine eyes?" the blind man replies, "I have told you already, and ye did not hear."[13] Later John ascribes a new status to the *possible*. No longer is it possibility in the logical sense, lodged between the true and the false (and distinguished from the false because non-contradictory). Nor is it possibility in the ontological sense, taking its place between being and non-being (Aristotle's "potential [*en-puissance*]"). It is, rather, *existential* possibility, such that we can tear away from ourselves as from our past and "abide outside of [*tenir hors*]" our condition, anterior or normative: *ex-sistere*. Such that it brings about the *unheard-of* in life.

From the start John speaks to the nature of this unheard-of eventuality "amid" which we find ourselves, and which therefore goes unnoticed: it is "life" (*zōḗ*, ζωή). The status of unheard-of eventuality, which thereby evades us even as it illuminates, is what John makes use of to think out life. For life is properly the unheard-of. Is this not its very definition? At the beginning of his prologue, moreover, John quickly takes us from the eventual "advened" ("All things advened by him") to its result, "the advened" (in the perfect: *gégonen*, γέγονεν) that is life. "The advened in him was life."[14] Life, in other words, is the deployed and continual effect of advent, unheard-of as it is. Thus life, even as it evades us in principle, is where light comes from: "and the life was the light of men."[15] John thinks of the positive and consistent status of becoming as advent so as to think out life as radically as he can. But how to grasp, how to find entry into, the thought of life? What is it to be effectively "alive"? "Christ" is for John not only he through whom becoming and being are joined but also he by whom advent promotes itself into life. It is through him that we can ponder how life can be alive.

IV

What is it to be alive?

It is because the eventual is revealed in life, or because life – through the mediation of "Christ" – results from the event's possibility, that life lies at the heart of John's thinking, and shapes the perspective throughout John's Gospel. Life is indeed the point of departure for his thought (at the start of the prologue). Event as advent is life. For life is the ever-new event with which becoming is pregnant when we no longer consider it, in the Greek manner, as a loss of being and – because shot through with non-being – as doomed to inconsistency. It is also becoming's result, its last word: "that ye might believe that Jesus is the Christ, the Son of God; and that believing ye might have life through his name"

(John 20; the next bit of text is held to be an interpolation). Life is genuinely the last word of John's thought inasmuch as the reason to have faith is to "have life in oneself." For to have life in oneself is the very definition of God, and of his Son, and links them: "For as the Father hath life in himself; so hath he given to the Son to have life in himself" (John 5).[1] The one and the other "quickeneth [make alive]"[2] (*zōopoieî*, ζωοποιειν); and this is, by the same token, the sole objective, the sole purpose, given to men: "that ye might have life."[3] Life is indeed not merely a condition: that of being alive. It is the absolute value. There is nothing, observes John, beyond life; or nothing can "get beyond" it [*la «dépasser»*]. Life can refer to nothing but itself. All things draw their meaning with respect to life, but life has meaning only with respect to itself. What distinction shall we make, then, between the minimal *being alive* [*être en vie*] and *having life in oneself* [*avoir en soi la vie*]? What separation shall we introduce within *life*, this most elementary of terms, so that it can rise from mere condition to vocation, and even the ultimate vocation?

The Greeks had already distinguished two kinds of "life" and given them different names.

On the one hand, qualified life (the "good" life), ethical and political life, life such as it is promoted within the framework of the polis and offers a choice between various kinds of life: the life they called *bios* (βίος). On the other hand, life in the sense of simply being alive, the sort that makes us (and Aristotle's God also) living beings: the life they called *zōé* (ζωή). The Gospel, however, does not take into account ethically or politically qualified life (life as *bios*) and adopts a different view of the separation to introduce within life, so as to think life through philosophically. Therein lies its novelty. On the one hand, John speaks of life in the sense of simply *being alive*, being animate, because possessing the vital breath. He calls this *psyche* (ψυχή; this relates to the Hebrew *nephesh*, though in Homer as well the warriors who die beneath the walls of Troy allow their *psyché*, their vital breath, to escape). On the other, John speaks of what he calls *zōé*, or *having life within oneself* in life's plenitude. He makes the distinction in the middle of his Gospel (10:10–11). It is his Gospel's heart. On the one hand, the shepherd "giveth his life" (sacrifices his life), his *psyche* (ψυχή), for his sheep. He is ready to die for them. On the other, he does this "that they," the others, his sheep, "might have life [which he now calls *zōé* (ζωή)][4] and that they might have it more superabundantly." "Superabundantly" rather than "abundantly" (the ordinary translation, *perisson* (περισσόν) meaning, as in Paul, an overstepping of the mark, a spilling-over, and surplus). Life is *superabundant*, as the multiplication of loaves is superabundant (whole basketfuls remain after the feast). This capital distinction, on which John builds his thinking, vanishes as soon as we read the Gospel in translation, which consistently renders as "life" what John conceives of in two separate terms. *Being alive* means two things. It might mean just *being alive*, as in the condition of not being dead; and it might mean *having life within oneself superabundantly*, or life insofar as it is alive, and thus cannot die: life as vocation. At least at first, John trains all his efforts on introducing the widest possible *divide* between the first and the second sense, and does so by expanding the field of the thinkable.

John opens such a divide between the two terms that, in one of his great passages, they can even repel each other: "he that loveth his life" – that is, cannot sever his attachment to it (to his "*psyché* (ψυχή)": to being alive) – "shall lose

42

it"; and "he that hateth his life in this world" – who can sever his link to life (still *psychē*), who can detach from it and not cling – "shall keep it unto life" – *zōē* – "eternal."[5] In other words, he who continues to adhere to his being-alive, and bogs down in it, shall lose his capacity to be fully – that is, superabundantly – alive. But he who can break free of an exclusive concern for his life can deploy that life as an effectively living life, a life such as can never die. This deployment, this exceeding [*dépassement*] of *psychē* to achieve *zōē*, of vital being to achieve full being – that is, super-abundant life – is unique to John. The other three evangelists, as we observe across their divide with him, never depart from the *vital*, from *psychē*, and never detach from it the *living*, *zōē*. "For who-soever will save his life [*psychē*] shall lose it; but whosoever shall lose his life [*psychē*][6] for my sake and the Gospel's, the same shall save it" (Mark 8:35; cf. Matthew 10:39 and Luke 17:33). In like manner Paul contrasts the body as vitality (the "psychical" body) and the body as spirituality, the "pneumatic" body. ("It is sown a natural body; it is raised a spiritual body" – 1 Corinthians.)[7] But he does not separate purely, properly *living* life from life that is merely *vital*. And so this, once he has conceived of the possibility of the event, and in what follows, is the second resource that John supplies. It becomes the chief and even unique question of life: what is it to "be alive," or how can I be fully – that is, effectively – alive, as this is the sole possible aspiration – the least abstract, constructed, artificial aspiration – that the living being that I am can have? In other words, how can I avoid languishing in the vital – in the slack [*étale*] – of my being-alive, and instead deploy life in me in its soaring [*essor*], in its gush and superabundance: that is, as the *source*[8] of life?

This is the question that the Greeks, thinking in terms of being, and later of knowledge, never asked – and that philosophy then set aside. The Greeks sought to understand the good life, in terms of *bios*, how one could live better, but never raised the more radical question of what it is to be effectively alive. Today, in our current retreat from religion, we have foolishly relegated this question to what we call "personal development," which sells a mixture of health advice and cheap spirituality that is in fact neither of the two. We have all watched P.D. thrive, and even bury philosophy with its non-books, but the question remains unanswered. Or else it permits a more serious, if not exotic, approach from the standpoint of Chinese thought, one of whose major themes is the matter of "nourishing [one's] life" (*yang sheng*, 养生). To *nourish life* as the Chinese understand it is not to feed one's "body" alone, or what would be the "soul," in the figurative and metaphorical sense of *nourish*, but to nourish one's vital potential. In more essential, or quintessential, terms, it is to feed one's breath and energetic capacity (*yang qi*, 养气). This instantly undoes the – now much-decried – mind–body duality (cf. my book *Vital Nourishment: Departing from Happiness*). John's relevance is precisely that, by separating *being-alive* (*psyché*) from *living* in the *primordial, absolute* sense (*zōé*), he hews strictly to the thought of life and can thus evade the old dualist trap – "body" and "soul" – into which Platonic Christianity falls. (But didn't Plato himself discover, having tried it in the *Phaedo*, that this dualism was just a convenience?) Thus John restores a certain standing and intelligence to the question that arises between the vital and the ideal: how to *promote* life within oneself. Such "life" is no longer properly biological, but neither is it metaphorical, in a figurative sense. It is life itself as life.

It seems to me, moreover, that John's distinction between sterile *being-alive* and life that is *absolutely alive* crosses over with Michel Henry's distinction (in *I Am the Truth*) between a "living entity" in the world, as treated by science, and what he calls "absolute phenomenological life" and Christianity has called God. Michel Henry's work, if we think it through, conjoins the thought of *immanence*, through which Life primordially engenders itself or comes into itself (in terms of *self-*: "self-revelation," "self-donation," "self-affection," etc.), with the thought of the *transcendental*, or Life's absolute Before with respect to all living entities that draw their capacity from it (in accordance with the status of *archi-* and the First: the Father, Archi-son, Archi-ipseity, Archi-generation, etc.). I wonder, though, whether Michel Henry might instead have opted to work through John's distinction between *psychē* and *zōē* – which I believe he never cites – and thereby prevented the discourse of phenomenology from, in a certain sense, closing in on itself and becoming strictly self-referential. Henry conceives of birth, for instance, strictly from the standpoint of "Life's self-generation as its self-revelation as the First living entity's essential Ipseity." To establish the first necessary distinction, to find our footing in the thought of life, the dissociation that John so discreetly introduces seems in this respect all the more operative.

I especially wonder whether, in thinking through the absoluteness of life in terms of the "transcendental," Michel Henry doesn't end up simply reversing the terms of traditional metaphysics – the phenomenological taking precedence, as it thereafter should, over the ontological – and consequently bringing back the old dualisms in accord with the irreducible opposition – restored to a *schism* – between "Life" and the "World" (the one's visibility being heterogeneous to the other's invisibility, and "birth" to "creation," etc.). If so, moreover, then Michel Henry can understand "ex-istence" only as the ego's futile "casting" of itself "out of its self" within the world, without ever reaching itself. He cannot understand "ex-istence" as the *existential* capacity to "abide outside of" – that is, outside of both itself and the world – so as to spill over the self and meet the Other. It is from this, it seems to me, that the subject achieves its primordial promotion. Michel Henry can therefore discuss the Other, in terms of mercy's "others," only at the end of his book, and then only as a secondary concern. Meanwhile, he is condemned along the way to condemn yet again – pell-mell, and in the name of Christianity – the "social sciences," "Freudianism," "modernity," "Galileo," etc. (p. 189). He thus gradually erects an undoubtedly defensive wall around himself, holing up in a Christian traditionalism that undermines the "Philosophy of Christianity" in his subtitle.

It seems to me, however, that this matrical distinction between insufficient being-alive and life that is effectively, absolutely living – the latter clearing its way [*venant à se dégager*] and promoting itself by divide [*écart*] with the former – is already laid out in Christ's dialogue with the Samaritan woman. The dialogue already puts the distinction to work. The well water that Jesus asks for is the water that sustains being-alive, at the level of *psyché*. Jesus thirsts and asks to drink of it. The water quenches his thirst, and then his thirst arises again, in keeping with the metabolism of the vital. Whereas the water that Christ can provide is "living water," in the sense of *zōé*, or, in the words of his interlocutor, who has perceived the distinction, "that living water" (*tò hýdōr tò zōn*, τὸ ὕδωρ τὸ ζῶν). This water, says Christ, "shall become"[9] ("shall advene," in the strong sense of the eventual), in whomsoever he gives it to, "a well of water springing up into everlasting life [*zōé*, ζωή]."[10] Christ passes pedagogically from the one to the other: from thirst-quenching water, the condition of being-alive, to the water that wells up within oneself, in which life primordially finds its *soaring* (its "source") and that quenches all aspiration for life. Later with his disciples, Christ passes in like manner from food brought from town to another food "that ye know not of," such that at harvest "he that soweth and he that reapeth may rejoice together," and such that it is stored "unto life eternal" (*zōé* once again).[11]

Moreover, because the theme of thirst-quenching water arises from the divide and tension between *psyché* and *zōé*, between being-alive and living life, I will not hasten to think of the one as the mere image of the other, as the commentators would have us do. "The water is made into a metaphor and becomes living water," says the excellent Zumstein, before summarizing the water's metaphorical interpretations. If, Zumstein continues, we conceive of the opposition between the waters as an opposition between the literal and the figurative sense, with the one becoming "the other's symbol," then we revert to dualism, as expressed in that same figurative/literal opposition. Moreover, we depart from John in failing to show that the one is nevertheless not cut off from the other, even as we allow its possibility to emerge by means of the divide with the other, and thereby achieve the transition from being-alive, with which we are ordinarily content, to effectively living being, soaring being, such as life can accede to. In fact, there is a return to being-alive at the end of the sequence (the first act of healing that Christ performs at death's approach). Or else might the two, in their very tension, start to join together with the laconic phrase "Thy son liveth"?

The Greeks taught us to *conceptualize*: that is, to go from the concrete plurality of things to a unitary idea that gathers ("subsumes") diversity into intelligibility. They taught us to raise our thinking from "beautiful things" to the beautiful itself: in other words, to the *idea* of the beautiful. This is the teaching of Socrates, in Plato and according to Aristotle, and opens the way to theoretical knowledge. Our evangelist, meanwhile, teaches us to *spiritualize*, which is something else entirely. In other words, he teaches us to deploy a spiritual dimension (is it merely a sense?) on the basis of the concreteness of things. In John this spiritual dimension blurs with the dimension that bestows life or "quickeneth [*fait vivre*]": from well water to "that living water." The "spirit" here is the breath-spirit that is blown into and spreads life (*pneûma*, πνεῦμα), not philosophy's spirit (mind)[12] of intellection and representation (*noûs*, voῦς). This is why *spiritualizing* does not reduce to *symbolizing*. We are not to go from an image to the thing of which the image is the image, as if well water were "symbolic" of the other kind. In other words, to spiritualize is not to exploit analogy so as to rise to an ideal, because the symbolism would once again set up an opposition between the intelligible and the sensible and thereby take us right past the livingness [*le vivant*] of life. In John, then, to *spiritualize* is to pass from the being-alive of beings (their *psychē̂*) to what makes them effectively alive (as *zōē̂*). This is why there is no symbolic *doubling* of meaning, as if we were to read the well water as the concrete image of an underlying abstract sense yet to be deciphered, like a double in intelligibility. What we have instead is a clearing out and opening up [*dégagement*]. From this well water that quenches thirst and preserves being-alive, an absolute import or dimension flares out and escapes,[13] by means of the divide with its concrete and limited determination, and this absolute import or dimension brings out, from itself, what is in itself the living life of which Jesus is both the revelation and the mediation in the Gospel of John.

Water turning into wine: that is, starting to detach from its determined and limited nature as water and becoming more precious (John 2, the wedding at Cana, the first "miracle"). Then well water that quenches thirst and preserves being-alive turning into water that quenches all thirst forever and promotes an eternally living life (*zōē*, John 4). Then manna that falls from heaven in the desert turning into the "bread of life" that is the flesh of Jesus Christ (John 6). There is a *spiritual*, and gradual, deepening, so as to approach what constitutes the livingness of life [*le vivant de la vie*]. In this respect John clearly distinguishes what is "flesh" from what is "spirit" (cf. the colloquy with Nicodemus, in John 3). Unlike Paul, however, he never sets the "letter" (the "flesh") in opposition to the spirit so as to condemn the flesh – death, purportedly – that the spirit might live.

John refrains from delving into the duality. As I have said, ideology is something he eschews. After laying out his reflections (and before announcing the Passion) he hews to the following essential thought: the spirit is what "quickeneth," and in this respect "the flesh profiteth nothing"; it is not a resource (John 6:63). Thus the spiritualness of the spirit and the livingness of life are the same thing. "The words that I speak unto you," Christ continues in John, "they are spirit, and they are life." This time, then, we have a resource: not to content ourselves with being alive but to seek a connection, within our lives, ever more diligently, with what "quickeneth." We must rise from the slack [*étalement*] of life to what might be its *soaring* [*essor*] and renders it effectively living, like a wellspring, a gushing "source." All ethics is henceforth nothing but a consequence of this. (This is why John never deals with *bios* (βίος).) Especially as this promotion of life is not the promotion of an *intensive* life, of the sort that modernity, with its Romantic heritage, celebrates in its deployment of the *vital*. It is the promotion of what, by divide, we might call *expansive* life, inasmuch as it gives of itself, shares itself, does not keep everything to itself, but devotes itself to the Other. In John this takes the form of the figure of Jesus, who *lives* by dying on the Cross for the lives of others.

But what are we to make of the "eternal life" (*zōē aionios*, ζωή αἰώνιος) in which living life is achieved? Life, we understand, cannot die, inasmuch as it is living. The life of the spirit, inasmuch as it is of "spirit," is not subject to the mortal condition to which being-alive is subject. There effectively exists an eternity of thought. We can read today a sentence written 3,000 years ago and understand it. We can also recall the primordial link in Greek between *aionios* in the sense of the eternal – before it was reconfigured as the "always being [*étant toujours*]" (*aeí-ón*, ἀεί ὄν) of metaphysics – and any organic liquid or fluid (tears, spinal fluid, etc.) that, already for the Greeks in Homer (as Richard B. Onians reminds us), expressed vitality; by opposition, death was desiccation. Yet John does speak of the "awak-ening" of the dead on the last day and of their resurrection, *anastasis*. Is this representation still tenable? Is it still useful? Yes, John has the merit of not making it into a bargain (better to sacrifice the brevity of this life for the eternity of the other) or a consolation. In fact, he at best only alludes to the Last Judgment. Is this the effect of mere cultural context (the ambient soteriology), or is it a dogma to underlie belief? The philosophy of the *resource*, meanwhile, can detach from this and even renounce it. As I have said, a resource exists only to the extent that we explore and exploit it. Thus we can choose to go no further and stop short of the Resurrection.

V

The logic of de-coincidence

Once we have understood the separation between minimal but sterile being-alive and life that is absolutely alive – between *psyché* and *zōé* – we must take a second, closer look at the formulation, the capital formulation, with which John puts it to work. We must do so if we are to perceive the singular logic that underlies life, or, to put things differently, that renders life living: "he that loveth his life [*psyché*] shall lose it; and he that hateth his life in this world shall keep it unto life eternal [*zōé*]."[1] What do the two opposed verbs, *love* and *hate*, mean? They are evidently not meant in a purely psychological sense, nor do they stem from a flat precept of asceticism. There is a schism between these two terms, *psyché* and *zōē*, and what it betokens is the coherence – albeit coherence by divide [*écartement*] – by which life is set in tension and promoted. To "love one's life" is to hold tight to one's being-alive, *psyché* – to cling to the vital, adhere to it, and mire one's life in it. "Hate one's life in this world," on the contrary, speaks to the need to peel away [*décoller*] from one's attachment to being-alive, restrained and conditioned as it is, and hoist oneself out of one's adaptation to one's world: that is, de-coincide with the adequation of (with) the *vital* in order to accede within oneself to *living* life. More generally, to *de-coincide* is to extract oneself from one's adequation-adaptation both to oneself and to one's world – "hate" one's life "in this world" – in order to redeploy the possibilities coiled within and reopen a future – i.e., an adventive becoming [*devenir d'avènement*] – to life. Such is the logic of the *living* in John's conception. If we do not de-coincide with our being-alive and with our world, if we are content and satisfied with them, then life in itself withers and goes sterile. Our positive adequation-adaptation with our being-alive and the world we live in, *by virtue of its very positivity*, amounts to a loss of our capacity for life, which becomes slack and fixed. We must therefore de-coincide with it, tear ourselves forcibly away from both its connivance and its coherence ("hate" it), so as to accede to the *livingness* of life.

From the start John founds this life-promoting logic of *de-coincidence* on God himself. John's first words read: "In the beginning was the Word, and the Word was with God, and the Word was God." The Word (the Logos) is in relation to God (*pros*, πρός: the preposition marking the relation) while at the same time being God himself. In other words, if he coincided with himself, knew no divide within himself, could not enter into a relation of exteriority with himself – in still other words, if he adhered to his being-alive – then God would lose his capacity to "make life" (*zōo-poieîn*). He would wither in his compact positivity and bog down as God. Thus God must *open a divide* with himself so as effectively to *advene* as his *living* self. Not only need God separate from himself so as to set himself outside himself, instead of remaining (resting) within himself, but he must extract himself from his adequation to his Godly nature so as to activate himself as God. God the Father must dispatch himself into the world as the Son. He, sovereign of Heaven, must make himself man suffering on earth. He, the Eternal, must undergo death on the Cross. Otherwise he will wither in his Godly essence. He must properly *de-coincide* with himself so as to *promote* himself into God. He must introduce the negative of internal dissent – must "hate," in human terms – so as to exercise his Godly capacity and *advene* eternally as the living God. (From this comes all of Hegel: to advene as oneself by "self-estrangement.") John's intellectual achievement – from which an essential Christian resource springs – is to understand that a self-coinciding God is a dead God. It is, on the contrary, by God's de-coincidence with himself that he is living and life-giving life.

Life promotes itself by de-coinciding with itself (better yet, life promotes itself as *zōḗ* by de-coinciding with its *psychḗ*). John gives us an exemplary statement of this in regard to Christ: "Therefore doth my Father love me, because I lay down my life, that I might take it again" (John 10:17). I "lay down" my life. In other words, I de-coincide with my being-alive, adapted (adopted) as it is to its life and its world, so as to further, so as to broaden, my capacity for life (by deploying it for others). To "lay down" my life is not merely to renounce or sacrifice it but, more essentially, to de-coincide with what, in the normal course of things, is subject to sedimentation (reification) in my life and results in its loss. The same goes for our relation to the Other, if we expect to have a *living* relation. In John (14:28) Jesus says: "I go away, and come again unto you" (*hypágō kaì érchomai pròs hymâs*, ὑπάγω καὶ ἔρχομαι πρὸς ὑμᾶς). It is by going away, by de-coinciding with the relation that I have with you, that I can come to you. Once again, we must translate the Greek literally, without projecting the meaning (here eschatological) we traditionally expect. For Christ does not now say "I will come again, and receive you unto myself," as at the beginning of the chapter.[2] He says something more radical, taking his words further, or, rather, expecting more from his listeners: I go away, *and* come again unto you. The *and* speaks laconically to the consequence. It is by de-coinciding with our established relation that I can effectively approach you. Who, indeed, can be unaware that it is by extracting myself from the *relation* I have established with the Other, which bathes in its adequation-adaptation (we know each other so well, are so well matched . . .), that I can once again *encounter* the Other?

60

Not just by taking my leave (as in the commonplace of absence) but by reopening a *divide* with the Other. The encounter occurs, then, in the intensive interspace [*entre*] that deploys between us. It occurs, that is, because I restore a distance, in proximity, that allows me to regain a perspective [*regard*] that discovers the Other, and consequently also to have some *regard*[3] for him. Through this I can make my relation with him a *living* one. Our relation is otherwise dead.

Moreover, we will better perceive the logic of de-coincidence, which is the logic of life, once we distinguish it from the logic of *inversion* [*renversement*], which is the traditional logic of religious conversion. The former is John's – yet we know that a resource, before it becomes amenable to sharing, must be singular to be a resource. The latter is more ideological in that it relies on inversion – the inversion of orders and values: from the world's order and values to their contraries, which we discover in God. As such this logic is common to the other evangelists and promoted by Paul the preacher. To "con-vert" (achieve salvation) is for Paul to turn the upside-down right-side-up: to turn "weakness" into "strength," the "spurned" into the "honored," the "obscure" into the "glorious," the "afflicted" into the "happy," etc. And primarily to turn the "folly" of the Cross, antithesis of Greek wisdom, into an eminently superior "wisdom." "For the wisdom of this world is foolishness with God" (1 Corinthians).[4] Or to go from the flesh to the spirit, from impurity to charity. In Paul, the inversion is itself connected with Christ's Passion and resurrection. By "emptying" himself Christ is exalted unto God; by humiliating himself he is elevated by God, etc. Paul grounds the Christian message in this logic of contraries. Salvation lies in an inversion-conversion such that, by faith, present wretchedness is commuted into future happiness. Death itself, at time's end, shall revert to life. The logic of life, however, is not polemical. It takes the contrary position to nothing: indeed, combats nothing (and is therefore not ideological). In like manner, it eschews rhetoric (magisterial in Paul, absent in John). For the negative is no longer to be found in the other or on the outside (the world, death). They are no longer to be denounced as such, in the world's filth or in sin's fall. The negative is to be found in life itself (as *psychē*): in the very manner in which life, by *attaching to* itself ("loving" itself), is itself *lost*. Life must therefore "die" to itself ("Except a corn of wheat fall into the ground and die . . ." (John 12:24)), must de-coincide with its enmiring, sterilizing adequation-adaptation, if it hopes to promote itself into life.

De-coincidence is in life – or, rather, is life itself. It is what makes life life, what allows it to *promote* itself into life. But to accede to life's inherent de-coincidence – to penetrate to the heart of John's account of Jesus' teaching – we must de-coincide also with the established discourse, which remains at the level of being-alive. Adherence to being-alive and adherence to the established discourse actually amount to the same *adherence*. This is why de-coincidence is so methodical. Better yet, since we must flank a difficulty that we cannot confront directly, this is why it is a *strategy*: the one Jesus employs with his successive interlocutors. In his dialogue with her, Jesus time and again takes up the words of the Samaritan woman, but does so to introduce a de-coincidence with her, to unhinge her,[5] as it were; to pry her from her adequation-adaptation; to open a divide and shift away – and thereby bring forth a new and unforeseen possibility: that of a "spiritual" or properly living sense. From well water to living water, from water that temporarily quenches thirst to water that quenches all thirst for all time, the de-coincidence introduced by Jesus takes effect within the speech of his interlocutor, so as to peel away from it and clear out [*dégager*] something that now takes on a whole other import. (The same thing occurs earlier, with Nicodemus.) Can Jesus in fact do otherwise? For he is always teaching us to seek detachment from the coherence (adherence) of the *obvious* (and especially from the coherence of being-alive) – that is, from what naturally "comes before" the mind – so that in the resulting divide we can come to understand a dimension of the absolute (the absolutely alive). In this respect de-coincidence is not critical (Jesus does not criticize his interlocutors), because criticism works on the supposition that interlocutors understand each other within the same perspective and apprehend the terms of the debate in the same way. This is not the case here. But neither is de-coincidence dissidence. Jesus opens no other way, offers up no other teaching. He teaches us to hear the same thing (life) differently (spiritually): we begin with our adherence to being-alive and pass on to what makes life life.

In a more general way, moreover, Christianity inherently effects a de-coincidence with Hebraism, though without separating from it. It undoes the coherencies established therein as truth and mired in their positivity: the once living but now sclerotic thought of the officials and Pharisees. As we all know, such ideological "coincidence" has always been the stuff of conformism. Jesus does not seek to break with the Jewish community – never dreams of such a thing – but does seek to change its perspective from within, so as to reopen a future for it. In this respect, criticism would have no purchase and achieve no result. We see this in the exchange (how could it be a "dialogue" if its purpose is to effect a shift?) about the bread of life (John 6).[6] When his interlocutors advance it as an argument Jesus takes up the theme of the manna sent to the Jews in the desert but does not exactly correct, contest, or even reinterpret it. Any such approach would place him on the same level as his interlocutors. Instead, he opens a hiatus with respect to the theme and thereby extracts it from what had hitherto been its co-herence, from a pertinence that had settled like silt. In this it "coincided." It is not that Moses gave the Jews this bread from the sky, in the literal – or, better yet, obvious – sense of the Biblical story; it is that my Father is giving it to you even today. Jesus steers the mind away from a factual truth (inasmuch as it is assignable and referable, and thus reassuring: "Moses") and towards a spiritual truth, which, as such, is always alive. Jesus proceeds in this manner throughout the exchange, bringing forth not a new meaning but a new ("spiritual") possibility of meaning, unperceived and, indeed, unintelligible from the previous perspective. He does not contradict the previous adequation. He drives a crack through it, gradually destabilizing it from the inside, and induces a sense of vertigo that opens the way to the unheard-of: it is I who am the bread of life.

This de-coincidence that reopens the possible from the inside, by peeling it away from the accepted coherence, is something that Jesus applies not only to his interlocutors' words but to his own as well. He takes successive passes, de-coinciding with what he has just said and thereby reopening it, withdrawing it from the understanding we have just formed, and venturing further with it. At one point (John 10)[7] Jesus begins with the banal image of a door: one must enter by the door and not by climbing over the wall; the good shepherd enters by the door. He then detaches the spirit from the established coherence, in de-coincidence with his stated theme, by advancing the notion that he is the door (through which one must pass to be saved). The "door" does not become properly symbolic (as we might be tempted to think, turning aside the difficulty), because the door through which the good shepherd passes is already understood to be figurative. There has been a displacement within the motif that, in the shift, hollows it out and internalizes it, detaches it from its objective, obvious comprehension, by subjectivizing it. This rattles the mind by stripping away its comfort, producing what I have previously called a sense of vertigo. The good shepherd is no longer he who goes through the door but he who makes himself the door. Jesus thereafter takes up the theme of the good shepherd once again, first in an obvious way: the good shepherd is he who "giveth his life" (lays it down) for the sheep. Then he immediately de-coincides with the motif: the good shepherd no longer lays down his life for the sheep, no longer sacrifices himself, but will "lay down [his] life that [he] might take it again."[8] For life must de-coincide with itself in order to promote itself into life. By successive de-coincidences Jesus teaches his interlocutor to steer away from one sort of intelligence – that of our adherence, both to the literal and to being-alive – so as to detect within it another sort, where the mind, by dis-adhering from what has bogged it down, makes available to us the unheard-of of the event [*l'inouï de l'événement*] – the event that is life: i.e., the event that is life inasmuch as life is alive.

And this, in John's Gospel, is indeed what Jesus does, by de-coincidence. He takes us from the *established* (sedimented truths), from the *obvious* (the meaning that comes naturally to mind because of its adherence both to the world and to being-alive), to the unheard-of. "Unheard-of" in the literal sense: what has never before been heard on the earth and Jesus' interlocutors therefore do not wish to (cannot) hear. Others speaking of Jesus: "This is an hard saying; who can hear it?" (John 6).[9] And Jesus speaking of himself: "ye cannot hear my word" (John 8).[10] What, indeed, could be more unheard-of than a man who claims to be God? And in John's Gospel Jesus does not back down from this claim, takes his intransigence to an extreme. To the point of provocation? "All that ever came before me are thieves and robbers" (John 10; when Jesus says he is "the door").[11] With respect to Jesus, in fact, and unlike the other evangelists, John does not write of the miraculous, or the strange, or the mysterious. Unlike Paul, he does not advocate an unacceptable logic so as to invert the accepted logic. He instead utters the unheard-of: the unheard-of of an event that is life, or of the event that is life inasmuch as it is alive. Here too, perhaps, we have a resource. Just as there is a resource in thinking that an event is possible (as an advent), there is a resource in thinking that one day something can be said that has never been said before: something that not only breaks with everything ever said in the past – breaks with the endless sifting of speech and defies all of thought's vassalage – but goes so far as to shatter the coherencies that seem most tightly sealed, down to the most tenaciously obvious notions (that death is dead). And can take such a risk.

Hence what is doubtless the strangest part of the story: that the thought of de-coincidence that inhabits and undergirds Christianity, at least in the Gospel of John, should have transformed into a dominant ideology, and recoiled into imposed coincidence; that a logic of de-coincidence like John's could become part of a dogmatic corpus; that this announcement of the unheard-of, running counter to the obvious and the established, could not only have become sedimented and sclerotic thought but also served to cement the oppressive apparatus of power that the Church became over the course of its history. It is not rare, in truth, for a system of thought that imposes itself ideologically to lead to its own perdition. China has taken Confucius' allusive, inchoate words, always varying, never slackening into a lesson or imposing themselves ("I would much rather not have to talk"[12]), and made it into the tiresome preaching of Confucianism, with its persnickety rules for living and stuffy conformism. With John, however, it seems to me we are dealing with a much more wide-ranging phenomenon. I wonder how the Church's dignitaries, and all who have called for an alliance of the throne and the altar, could actually have read John. Just how far can meaning be perverted? Does it suffice to say that the Church, in compromising itself with the reigning powers, betrayed John? Should we perhaps see in this the paroxysm of what Marx said about the dominant ideology and its power of inversion?

Or might it *also* be that John's text contains the reversal within it already? Might John's Gospel itself, like any text taken to its limit, incur its own fragile ambiguity? While hazarding the unheard-of, and in order to hazard it, might John's Gospel be led to pass – be reduced to passing – from that extreme into anathema: to allow eminent openness to tip into sectarianism, the adventurous into exclusion (excommunication)? "All that ever came before me are thieves and robbers."[13] Might not the most daring meaning here inevitably amount to a condemnation of others? Might this not be the price that vertigo must pay in order to find its footing and assurance? In order to find a new vis-à-vis, a normalcy, but of the most tightly closed sort? Might the flipside of de-coincidence be intolerance? To form a judgment on this we must investigate the nature of truth in John's Gospel: of Jesus' saying he is the truth before saying he is life.

VI

Reconfiguration of truth

The statement of the following is capital, properly unheard-of: "I am the way, the truth, and the life" (John 14:6). It is also laconic, the mere succession of terms conveying both their gradation and a passage from one to the next, like steps to be climbed: the way – the truth – the life. The first lesson from this is that truth is for life. Or let us say instead that truth is no longer the last word; life itself is. Truth is the way to "life." What is being said here is not some banality: that truth is useful for life, or even that truth is dethroned from its speculative use (for knowledge) and has a practical use. What is being said, rather, is that the truth's very vocation is to open the way to life inasmuch as life is alive. Not the "true life" described in everything from Plato to Augustine, such as subjects life to the criterion of truth, or at least places it in truth's shadow, but life inasmuch as it is its own principle or "source" (*zōḗ*, ζωή). Once that is established, the thing to retain is that truth is to be considered not in the down-stream [*dans l'aval*] (of predication) but in the upstream [*dans l'amont*] (of enunciation). Truth must be traced back to an "I" and set forth as the prerogative of that "I." Truth no longer refers back to content: this is the truth. What now con-stitutes truth is a subject. Through Christ's status, truth becomes the subject's act. The way had, of course, been laid for this violent mutation of truth's status: I am "the bread of life" (John 6);[1] I am "the light of the world" (John 8);[2] I am "the door" (John 10).[3] The subject – and not some authority, or the world, or the past – is set forth, at the start, as self-sufficient grounds. Henceforth nothing, in rank or in time, precedes the emer-gence of this Subject who says "I." Not that we must now think of truth as subjective and defy-ing the demands of objectivity (like Feuerbach interpreting miracles). Rather, truth is now *sub-jectivized*. In other words, it is placed under the condition of the being-subject, who in Christ is raised to the absolute. The result is a complete reconfiguration of what "truth" can be, a reconfiguration of capital import, because it raises new possibilities for the thought of existence.

The first consequence is a de-theorization of truth, and a deepening of the divide with philosophy. Because truth depends on the subject, John can speak of he who "doeth truth." A potent phrase drawn from the Septuagint: "But he that doeth truth cometh to the light" (John 3:21). The truth is no longer like a transcendent given that we open ourselves up to by submission. Instead, the subject, through his behavior, "carries it out" or "makes it" – that is, makes it advene. Thus the truth "shall make you free" (John 8:32). Not only does the truth free us from the servitude of sin, in morality's traditional formulation, but "make free" takes on a new meaning, in relation to life: it signifies positively that the truth will offer itself up as a "dwelling" in which to live. Thus, also, truth, dissociated from theory, is associated with "grace" (which fills: John 1),[4] as well as with the "spiritual," which, in clearing away [*dégageant*] adherences both literal and vital, is identified with what is absolutely alive. Nowadays we are put off by such terms (*grace, the spiritual*, etc.), but we must come to understand how they detach the truth from the speculative, cause it to spill over on various sides, and seek to convey (to what point is this possible to convey?) a truth that *quickens* [*fait vivre*]: when the relation of truth to life is no longer a matter of (external) *application*, and thus of foisting (as in morality's "rules for life"), but of (internal) *promotion* – the truth illuminating life itself in its capacity to be alive. This impugning of the common, anchored conception of truth culminates at the end of the first exchange between Jesus and Pilate (at the end of John 18). Truth stems no longer from having (knowledge) but from being. To be "of the truth," says Jesus; to proceed from it as a subject (*ho òn ek tēs alētheías*, ὁ ὢν ἐκ τῆς ἀληθείας). One must originate in the truth in order to live. Caught off guard, Pilate replies: "What is truth?" Not "What is the truth?" or "What is a truth?" as in the ordinary trans-lation,[5] with its convenient article and refusal to question anything beyond truth's definition. Instead we get a far more radical question: what is "truth"? What can "truth" signify if it draws its authority from the subject as such?

Because it is the subject, in its Christly status, that lies at the root of truth, and because truth is no longer to be conceived in its conformity with being, as in Greek philosophy, the entire affair (as we might speak of a police inquiry) in John's tale is to identify this Subject. To *identify* it from others' point of view; to *reveal* it from the self's. If we view *oneself* in terms of the schism between *same* (*idem*) and *self* (*ipse*), as described by Levinas (in *Otherwise than Being*) and Ricœur (in *Oneself as Another*), then in John's Gospel the divide between same and self deepens to the point of incompatibility. For the question of *others* is the question of *idem* or *identity*. Already with respect to John the Baptist we read: Art thou the Christ?[6] Art thou Elias? Art thou the prophet? (John 1:19–21). Because this line of questioning reaches a dead end we must turn to the question of *ipse*: "What sayest thou of thyself?" In like manner Jesus is spoken of throughout the Gospel as follows: "Is this not Jesus, the son of Joseph, whose father and mother we know?" (John 6:42). Or, later: "as for this fellow, we know not from whence he is" (John 9:29). Identity as such is differential (established by distinction from others) and referential (referring back to a common genre from which difference is established) while also being fixative: my identity is the part of me that should not change, as noted in my identification card. This is, however, superficial, because it says nothing of me as I myself am, as a subject, as *ipse*. Moreover, such identity always requires verification. Those who encounter Christ after his death must identify him once more. Mary at first mistakes him for the gardener.

Moreover, the others in John's Gospel (the crowd, the Pharisees, Pilate, etc.) are always wondering about the *identity* of this Jesus individual, whereas Jesus himself time and again replies – in irreducible de-coincidence – with his *ipseity* as a subject: what he is in himself, the Christ. *Ipseity* denotes the absolute singularity of the subject *such as he is in himself* and such as the world cannot reach him. Not that the subject holds it back, or seeks to keep it secret. Rather, ipseity is the part of the subject that cannot stand on equal footing with the world. It is therefore what escapes the correlation of the subjective with the objective, the correlation that Feuerbach allowed himself in explaining Christianity – and that doomed his explanation to failure. Ipseity is not something to be distinguished from others; it can be revealed only from within itself and its own unicity. The Gospel of John is thus the gradual self-revelation of the *ipseity* of Jesus as the Christ, for only the self can say of itself who it is as a "self" (αὐτός, *autós, ipse*). No one can do it for me or in my name. In this sense the reversal of the matter of identity into ipseity in the person of Christ is exemplary. All we do is utter our ipseity, what we are in and of ourselves, become as our ipseity is, and do so despite the identifications that are continually being projected and affixed onto us. We never stop claiming our ipseity. We see Rousseau telling the tale of his *Confessions* with the sole purpose of expressing, or proclaiming, his ipseity, buried as it is beneath all the identities with which others have imperturbably covered it. In fact, we can only "proclaim" our ipseity, because it is never acknowledged, forever masked as it is by identification.

An identity reducible in this manner to the "same" of *idem* is all the more impossible to fix for the subject Christ. It is all the more worthy of scorn because, by John's notion of an extremely singular Christianity, and before the rulings of any council, Christ is already both totally man and totally God; he is thus not *identifiable*. This is a matter of principle. By his ipseity Christ lifts the opposition between these contraries that would identify him. Rather than confound them, he dis-excludes them. And not by the more or less developed but common way of the history of religions, the way of deification (Roman emperors too became gods upon their death), but by the inverse way of God, who does not meddle with men, like the gods in Homer, but becomes fully human: or is *born* man (the "incarnation"). On the one hand, then, Jesus completely takes on human pathos – in the Passion – and knows no impassivity or "ataraxia," the traditional mode of elevation to wisdom, in Greece as in China (in Stoicism as in *Mencius, bu dong xin*, 不动心): "Now is my soul troubled" (John 12; and already in John 11, with the death of Lazarus). In this he denounces the great foisting of much-celebrated impassivity, which is not more-than-human but inhuman: Jesus at Gethsemane in the Gospels of Matthew and Mark, or even Matthew and Mark's accounts of Christ's final words: "My God, my God, why hast thou forsaken me?"[7] What these speak to is worse than doubt; it is despair.

On the other hand, and *at the same time*, Jesus in his Christly ipseity proceeds completely from the absolute and from the eternity of God. John is more insistent here than his fellow evangelists, as we can see from the start, when he presents Jesus as the Logos with respect to God. He "was" before the world "advened." The two qualifications actually meet. Upon hearing others acknowledge him as the "Son of God" (e.g., Nathanael early on, in John 1) Jesus calls himself the "Son of man," though he does so here to denote his timeless communion with and in God. And this, by its very contradiction, without our projecting any eschatology onto it, implodes the two categories, these two most immovable of categories. Not only is the question of identity undone but, through Christ's mediation, the separation is lifted between the ipseity of man and the ipseity of God. The deepest of John's thought concerns the manner in which in the Christ, *in Christo*, the ipseity of man, of every "self," is called to end its isolation from (to commune in) the ipseity of the Other (God), whose welcome is indefinite. This announces a promotion of humanity in its very humanity, itself opening the way to the secular – but never completely secularized – notion of "progress": a notion alien to Greek thought.

What matters is not that Christianity might have ascribed superior or supreme or even absolute value to "Man," as has often been said. That would still be ideological. What matters is that, in the figure of Christ, Christianity has put forth the absolute ipseity of the subject: when Jesus takes up the Septuagint's phrase of divine revelation, saying nothing but "I am," *ego eimi*, ἐγὼ εἰμί – this time with no predicate appended (John 8:24, 13:19). This is the unheard-of ipseity of Jesus as the Christ. But isn't every other ipseity from then on revealed to be unheard-of, by the sole virtue of being *ipseity*? For the important thing isn't just to have put forth, through Christly status, an "I" subject at the start (in the prologue: "The Same was in the beginning with God") but to have put it forth as "being." It is an "I" in its ipseity that "is" *being*: "I am." And then – instead of making being into Being, as in the ontology of the Greeks – to have made the ipseity of the self into absolute, authentic being. Hence the "self" of "I am," in its ipseity, separates radically from any *ego* (from ego-ism). Hence too the nature of the *promotion of the human* that occurs in Christianity begins to come into focus. The purpose was never to encompass all reality within the perspective of "man" or to have it depend on him, as when the Greeks (Protagoras) called man "the measure of all things" ("and of the existence of things that are, and of the non-existence of things that are not"),[8] and thus to make "man" the "measure" of Being, and by such relativism to lay radical grounds for "humanism." The purpose, rather, was to recognize (promote) the self-subject of ipseity (in Christ) as Being's absolute: "I am." But what results from erecting the self-subject, in its ipseity, into an absolute is a double reconfiguration of truth. On the one hand, we have a whole other way of relating to truth, as expressed by a new meaning of the word *believe*. On the other, correlatively, we have a whole other status for its pertinence. Truth is no longer demonstrated; it is "witnessed." *Believe* and *bear witness*, two verbs that recur throughout the Gospel of John, meet in a common – and total – engagement of the self of ipseity.

Because it involves ipseity – selfness in itself – *believe* takes on a whole other meaning. "Believe in" (*pisteúein eis*, πιστευειν εἰς), John often writes. And, in fact, everything rides on the shift from "believing that" [*croire à*] to "believing in" [*croire en*].[9] What we believe when we *believe that* is from the start limited, constrained, objectivized (even when the belief is that God exists). But *believing in* – i.e., in a self, in an ipseity – is not undefined but infinite. When I say "I believe in you" I have no limit in view. Moreover, *believing that* can be detailed and itemized: I can believe that X is and not that Y is, and thus make a selection. But *belief in* is by necessity whole; it calls for an absolute. When I say that I believe in you I no longer wonder "what" in you I believe in. To put things differently, *believing that* entails a necessary measure of credulity, even if I have good reason to believe, because I might just as easily not believe what I believe. I recognize its hypothetical character (e.g., belief that Santa Claus exists).[10] Whereas *belief in* is not credulous but trusting. By the phrase "believe in yourself" – one that a parent might say to a child, or vice versa, or that one lover might tell another – I mean that I am counting on you, that I am expecting something of you, that I am placing my hopes in you, in you as yourself, in your ipseity, or that I am expecting everything of you. Thus *belief in* entails a self, an ipseity, on both sides. When I *believe in* someone I involve the entirety of myself. What I *believe in* in the person in whom I believe is what he himself reveals of himself, but also what he conceals within. *Belief that* might be open to convincing, but its truth will still rest on insufficient grounds; I would prefer knowledge that was certain. But the truth of *belief in*, precisely because it entails an as-in-oneself, will not be measured by a truth subject to proof; it is its own guarantee and can claim no other. You must believe in me, says Christ, and not believe what they say of me. But hasn't the Church, with its dogma, been compelled to shift from *belief in* (ipseity) to *belief that* (identity) – and made the latter into the "faith" that tempers its armor?

Like *believe*, *bear witness* entails the self as the self of a subject. The two verbs respond to and confirm each other, for a truth can be either demonstrated or witnessed. In the former, the truth remains external to the subject's self and makes use of it, counting on the sheer universality of its reasons to convince. Belief is what philosophy lays claim to: "those who hear, not me, but the universal Reason [*discours-raison*, logos] . . .," says Heraclitus.[11] When it comes to bearing witness the truth is not so much internal to the subject – like a strictly subjective truth – as borne, or "taken on," by the subject in his absolute position as a subject. The subject commits himself entirely, as a self, in his ipseity, by affirming it (to affirm it). As with belief, we can bear witness only by committing ourselves entirely. As with belief, bearing witness cannot be divvied up and ascribed solely to the witness or to what is witnessed. We cannot bear witness halfway. It is this *witnessed truth* that John lays claim to. From the beginning to the end of his Gospel, *bear witness* (*martyreîn*, μαρτυρεῖν) is the iterative verb that designates the sole possible grounds for Christianity's truth – grounds that instantly negate the rational discourse of "proof." John the Baptist bears witness to the coming of Christ, Christ bears witness to his Father, his Father bears witness to him, his works bear witness to him, and his disciples will in turn bear witness. In sum, Christianity's strength is to have grounded itself in the fact that the unheard-of, precisely insofar as it is unheard-of, and thus beyond all imagination (which always consists strictly of the known and the finite), cannot be invented. The unheard-of as in the affair of the Christ. All we could ever do is bear witness to it, because only the power of an ipseity's involvement – and the revelation thereby of an ipseity in its sovereignty – can legitimate the claim.

The result is a change in meaning. We have first the strictly juridical sense of *bear witness*, as understood in both the Jewish and the Greco-Roman worlds – a case in point being the meticulous discussion about whether Christ can bear witness to himself (John 5).[12] From this a sense that reveals itself to be *existential* clears its way out and emerges [*se dégage*], precisely because it involves the subject's entire self, in its ipseity. Bearing witness takes it for granted that this truth cannot exist without my testimony. Without me it would not be. How many throughout history have done everything they could, heroically, to survive (in concentration camps, under threat of extermination) so as one day to bear witness: that is, to ensure, thanks to their testimony alone, that what has actually occurred is forever affirmed and not denied or erased? Thus *bearing witness* is intrinsically tied to events. An event takes on the dimensions of an *event* only inasmuch as testimony is adduced for it. At the same time, however, the truth in question calls on the subject to bear witness to it, to bear witness against all opposition, with his entire self. It calls on the subject all the more radically in his ipseity. It calls on his deepest self, and thereby uncovers something deeper than the self. For this very reason it promotes the witness into a subject, such that he will no longer be restrained or reduced by the world's imposed conditions. To bear witness under torture. To "bear witness" to the point of death: "martyrdom." Such that, by his testimony in defiance of, or at least in refusal to submit to, the world, the subject can "abide outside of" the world – outside of a world closed in on its power struggles – and, by no longer coinciding with that world, properly "ex-ist."

VII

Ex-istence: to dwell in the Other by abiding outside of the world

In essence, John's Gospel concerns the subject's capacity to abide outside of the world within the world, and thereby promote itself into an *ex-isting* subject, because from then on it exceeds the world's measure. We therefore find in it hardly any psychology or anthropology. Because he recognizes human pathos in the Passion of the Christ, John conceives of the "heart" (*kardía*, καρδία) as the sole locus of inner sorrow. The Greeks, meanwhile, recognize only the heart of the *thymós*, which lies between the activities of desire and thought, and is vested with the vital force that deploys as "courage." In announcing Christ's death John makes the heart the locus of infinite sorrow (John 14:15), but he does not develop the notion into the capacity to react to the suffering of others, a capacity whose "sclerosis" other evangelists denounce as a "hardening of hearts" (*sklērokardía*, σκληροκαρδία). Nor, more importantly, does John make it the new locus for the apprehension of faith. In Paul, by contrast, the "eyes of your heart"[1] open to revelation, just as in Plato the "eye of the soul"[2] holds theoretical knowledge. Indeed, John does not establish a new vision of man in the manner of Paul, who posits a double – the "outward" man, fated to decrepitude, and the "inward" man, reborn in faith – and observes as man is dramatically torn apart: the starting point for the great thematic deployment of Europe's inner conflict of conscience. It is in Paul that "conscience" (*syneídēsis*, συνείδησις) emerges, beyond comprehensive knowledge (the *sýnesis*, σύνεσις, of the Greeks), to denote the inner tribunal – indeed, the most intimate such tribunal – where both the capacity to "bear witness" (Romans 1) and the subject's inalienable liberty (1 Corinthians) originate. John, for his part, is attentive in the figure of Christ chiefly to the Subject's self-revelation in his unheard-of ipseity.

Because he distrusts identification (always

externally practiced and externally applied), and because the only truth logically to be expected comes from the self-revelation of an ipseity (especially from Christ or from life itself as an event – Hegel would say from reason), John stands carefully aloof from any moral structure. He does not hold forth on values, or separate good from evil. He gives us no sermon on the Beatitudes, no evocation of Hell, no dramatic Judgment scene. Not even a great plea. Paul's potent inversion of the law by faith boasts the strength of its forceful argument but also, consequently, suffers the weakness of all assertion. As I have said, John does not partake of ideology – or partakes as little as possible. He approaches morality, rather, from the negative angle, on the basis of what is not, or engages his search for it in the direction suggested by its absence. For morality will not be prescribed. It too is the object of a self-revelation.

We see this in the episode of the adulterous woman and the near-silence in which it plays out. It is true that critics have long considered the episode a late interpolation. Opening suddenly before us is a vast corpus of exegetical knowledge, built on centuries of rigorous reading of the passage and rejection of its authenticity. The passage has nevertheless come into its own within the Gospel of John. That it has found its place, even as an interlude, attests to its coherence with the rest. Faced with a trap in the form of a dilemma (either he abides by the Law and condemns the woman, thereby renouncing mercy, or else he retains his mercy and betrays the Law), Jesus continues writing on the ground, not getting involved. Then, famously, he says, "He that is without sin among you, let him first cast a stone at her,"[3] thereby evading the judgment the world has locked itself into. In escaping the alternative, this cry bores a hole in the system of that world, and from this point on we see no way to lay blame. Because he refrains from preaching, Christ deflects criticism. Because he does not moralize, stays beyond the pros and the cons the world shuts us (and itself) into, takes no side, but undoes the partiality of sides, a morality can at last proceed from itself. At last a morality – as is exceedingly rare – needn't be open to suspicion (thanks to its self-revelation). And thus this somewhat clandestine passage in the Gospel is an infinite *resource*. The scene has so often been painted.

Yet in one respect John does seem to slide into ideology, and of the most off-putting kind:

his apparent rejection of the world as a negative totality and as dregs of the divine. This is why Christianity has fallen into such neglect today. "Me it [the world] hateth"; "the works thereof are evil";[4] "ye are of this world; I am not of this world."[5] But "I have overcome the world."[6] Modernity, however, has rightly spat out any ideal world that uses the illusion of an Elsewhere to slander this world, the real world, the only world, the only real one. Although he says in John's Gospel that he is "from above,"[7] that he is "come into the world," and then that he will "leave the world"[8] and return to the Father, Jesus does not say in John's Gospel that there exists another world that doubles and devalues this one, as metaphysics (or ideologized Christianity) has unfortunately said. In John's Gospel, moreover, "world" is rife with ambivalence. I "spake openly" to the world;[9] the world too is an "event" of God's; for "God so loved the world. . . ."[10] Once again John's words proceed negatively and convey their teaching by implication: "I am not of this world." And just what is it "not to be of this world"? Or what is it to *abide outside of* it? Must it amount to rejecting and condemning the world? Rather than an imperative to flee the world, to escape it, might we not see in this the ferment of a philosophy of ex-istence? To state it in reverse (positively), can a subject keep himself completely *in* the world? Doesn't his "as himself," his as-*ipse*, already and necessarily tear a hole in the world's never-to-be-unknotted skein, if only because he contains within himself a possible self-revelation that can never find its place there?

To address this question we must head further upstream. Once it puts itself forth as a subject, once it says "I" (utters the "I" of "I am"), doesn't a self necessarily open a breach in the world? By simply saying "I," the "I" that reveals a "self," do I not cause my *self* to emerge from the finite, encompassing whole that is the world? From the ipseity that is mine, and that rails against all the identifications that this world walls us in with, can I help fissuring the satisfied completion of the world, showing just how mired it is in its compactness? Do I not *dis-adhere* from this world every time I say "I" and thereby reveal myself? Once I put myself forth as a subject, in my ipseity, *I* can no longer be completely of the world. *Ipseity* is what cannot belong to the world: Jesus says as much in the Gospel of John when he invokes his "royalty." Not properly speaking (properly translating) "my kingdom," the flat (sterile) locative of the standard version,[11] but instead "my royalty," or "the royalty that is mine" (*hē basileía hē emḗ*, ἡ βασιλεία ἡ ἐμὴ), a more rigorous and adversarial phrase that speaks not to possession but to power, and signals that the subject is enunciating his position – "sovereignty" – as subject. By invoking "the royalty that is mine" Jesus aims in the Gospel of John essentially to give salience to his position – his sovereignty – as a Subject that can now, in his ipseity, no longer be a vassal to the world. Might this not be, through such Christly sovereignty, the position of any subject extracting himself from the world strictly by revealing himself in his ipseity as a subject? "They are not of the world, even as I am not of the world" (John 17).[12] And might this not be definitively, in a non-ideological but effective way, the universality of Christianity?

What the "royalty" that is Christ's and is not of this world means as a *resource* in the Gospel of John is that the subject necessarily *de-coincides* with the world in affirming – or, better yet, self-revealing – his ipseity. But also that the subject thereby "ex-ists," abiding outside of the world's enclosure, in non-integration. He can therefore effectively "bear witness" – against the opposition that the world can impose or solely against the world's judgment. It is by *ex-isting* in this way that he can pass from *psychē*, his attachment to his vital being in the world, to *zōē*, life that is "superabundant," because effectively exceeding the world's measure. Thus we have *in* the world, as Jesus is in the world, what does not belong to – is irreducible to – the world. We have, in its most literal expression, "ex-istence." The subject is not complicit in or compromised by the world; more radically, he cannot coincide with the world. This confers on him, in his ipseity, his initiative and dignity as a subject. The "dignity" of a subject, stemming from his ipseity, at last takes on meaning. But this is not the dignity of a mere self; it is also concomitant with the Other. There is no "you" to face a self unless that "you" is also extracted from the world. We must abide at least slightly outside of the world, not allow ourselves to be confined by it, not become its vassals, if we are to exist in our ipseity, and the Other, also detaching from the world, from anonymous other-dom, must exist *at the same time* in his ipseity as Other. As Levinas says, a face is not of the world. In both us and the Other, an ipseity always brings to light an exteriority within the world. Jesus does not call forth another world when, in the Gospel of John, he claims before Pilate a royalty that is not of this world. He instead opens another dimension within this one: or, more properly stated, he opens the dimension of the Other. In other words, it is impossible to encounter the Other *in* this world. Should either of us, the Other or I myself, be only in this world, then we are each enclosed in our respective solitude.

To understand John, then, we must link the *existential* capacity to abide outside of the world to the *ethical* capacity to abide near the Other – or, in John's even more radical formulation, to abide *in* the Other. What John so forcibly says is that I must abide outside of the world, must extract myself from the partitioning of both its individuations and its identifications (the two go hand in hand), so that I might inhabit the Other in myself, in my ipseity. Or, to state the converse, I must be *outside of* the world to be *inside of* the Other, to inhabit his ipseity. "Being" in the other, "dwelling" in him, is, in fact, John's great theme, and it dispenses him from morality: "I am in the Father, and the Father in me" (John 13–15).

This capacity to *be in the other* is something Jesus shares with the others: "ye in me, and I in you."[13] "In" the other, in infinite extension of one's ipseity. Already, as the theme of Jesus' body offered up as the "bread of life" draws to a close, we read: I live "through the Father"[14] and "he that eateth me, even he shall live by me" (John 6).[15] "Through": that is, on the inside and throughout, in an *expansive* motion proper to life itself. Those who are dear to me live effectively "through" me. Neither forced nor figurative, the expression shows how far the existential deployment of life can go. John makes it the condition of what we might literally call *the intimate* [*l'intime*]: I dwell in you and you in me, in the "deepest part" of you and in the "deepest part" of me (*intimus*) – that is, in the deepest part of (deeper than) each of us, precisely because we have emerged from our belonging to the world where we each have lived, in the sense of *psychē*, confined within our selves or to our in-ourselves. This *exteriority* with respect to the world is thus the condition of a shared *interiority* between the other and the self. For only in abiding outside of the world can I extract the other from the power struggles that make up the world. In other words, only in this way can I extract him as he is in himself, as *ipse*, and stop projecting my interests onto him. Only in this way can I begin to encounter him effectively and, John would say, "love" him.

But we must yet work to dispel the great confusion over love, which the Gospel makes into the sole commandment: "that ye love one another" (John 15:17). The Gospel promotes "love," *agápē*, ἀγάπη, in a radically new sense, as the vector of the intimate, with no relation to altruism. And yet I am surprised to see the Greek term *agápē* translated now as "love," now as "charity." (Before we had the reverse: the same word, *life*, serving to translate two Greek words, *psyché* and *zōé*, that John took pains to distinguish.) "Charity" steers us towards virtue, whereas "love" (*agápē*) lies upstream from all virtue and dispenses us from it. Once more, then, we must translate literally. Paul does not say, for example, "follow the path of love" (Ephesians)[16] as in the standard translation, which has already worn a rut. He says, "roam every which way, come and go in love" (*peripateîte*, περιπατεῖτε). In Christianity *agápē*, in unitary fashion, means love in its *expansive* sense – that is, in the sense of expansive life, signified by *zōé* – as opposed to love in the possessive

98

sense: that of intensive life, conferring its full possible deployment on vitality alone. Expansive love is the love of "I live through you," as it spreads limitlessly throughout, from the ipseity of the one to (into) the ipseity of the other, and uncovers the ipseity of the one to that of the other in such a way that they will not be contained in the world. Unlike possessive love, then, expansive love "envieth" not, is not "puffed up," "seeketh not her own," etc. (1 Corinthians).[17] For such love is what pervades and undoes the separation between beings, undoes their isolation in the world, and allows each to "dwell" in the other. Otherwise we end up with "love one another" and lose the resource; we end up with a phrase that vindicates Nietzsche, who denounces it as the craven, gregarious shrinking of those (the "weak") who have refused to face solitude and its heroic destiny.

Such love is a resource because it promotes an absolute – not in the (philosophical) Greek way, where *érōs* (ἔρως) raises limited, specific, physical desire to the (universalizing) desire for ideas – but through what is revealed thereby as the ipseity of a singular subject. Thus I consider "Christian" – that is, produced or made possible by Christianity, and by neither Greek nor Chinese: that is, nowhere to be found in those contexts of thought – this woman's reply, many analogues of which exist in European literature (this one is taken from de Maupassant's *Mont Oriol*): "In a steady voice, with a tender and resolute air, she said: 'I belong to you body and soul. Do with me what you will.' She then took her leave, allowing him no reply." To make a gift of oneself, and make that gift as whole as possible, from one's most intimate self, one's deepest recess. John, who, unlike Paul, does not theorize "love," stages it powerfully. (That the scene might be apocryphal makes it no less valuable from the resource perspective.) The last scene. Jesus asks, "Peter, lovest thou me [from *agápe*, ἀγάπη]?"[18] He specifies: "more than these?" Even disinterested love will call for a predilection to attest to it. Peter, not daring to resort to the absolute-promoting term *agápe* (ἀγάπη), retreats to the affectual and replies: "Thou knowest my affection for thee"[19] (that I "cherish" you: *philō se*, φιλῶ σε). Not "Thou art dear to me" or "I love thee," but you yourself know that I love you. There is no need for me to tell you; you know it within yourself, in your ipseity.

Or consider the opening of the scene where Jesus washes his Disciples' feet. Jesus, "having loved his own which were in the world, he loved them unto the end." *Unto the end* (*eis télos*, εἰς τέλος). If we love with expansive love, in the sense of *agápē*, we do indeed love to the end. Unto the end, which is not death. For this end, *télos*, refers not only to a temporal end but also to accomplishment, completion, fulfillment, or full development. Love's accomplishment and full deployment are not in fact complete until the Other has died. This applies first of all to Christ, the foundation of "Christianity" in its history. Not by belief in the resurrection but by divide with the vital and its life, it is only after the Other's death that the Other – any Other – begins to be loved fully with expansive love.

Translator's notes

I Refusal to avoid (the question of Christianity)

1 *Advene* (*advenir*) and *advent* (*avènement*) are special terms in the author's philosophical lexicon, and tie in with his notions of the divide (*écart*) and, especially, of *ex-istence*, wherein a subject that is *truly alive* abides outside of the world, while remaining within it. This is the whole point of the book. An advent here is an occurrence that comes from outside of the world.

2 The first two lines of Louis Aragon's poem "La Rose et le Réséda," a call to put religion aside in the resistance against the Nazis.

3 A reference to Henri Bergson's "supplément d'âme" (literally *supplement of soul*) – "We must add that the body, now larger, calls for a bigger soul, and that mechanism should mean mysticism": Henri

Bergson, *Two Sources of Morality and Religion*, trans. R. Ashley Audra and Cloudesley Brereton, London: Macmillan and Co., 1935, p. 310.

4 Ludwig Feuerbach, *The Essence of Christianity*, trans. Marian Evans, London: John Chapman, 1854.

5 "Then Jesus said unto him, Except ye see signs and wonders, ye will not believe."

6 Standard French and English translations differ in their choice of synonym. The French word *essence* figures in, for example, Ludwig Feuerbach, *Essence du christianisme*, trans. Joseph Roy, Paris: A. Lacroix, Verboechoven & Cie., 1864; the English word *nature* in Ludwig Feuerbach, *The Essence of Christianity*, trans. Marian Evans, New York: Calvin Blanchard, 1855.

II Resources

1 *Soaring* [*l'essor*] is a special term in Jullien's lexicon and stands in opposition to *slackness* or *spread* [*l'étale*]. What soars is alive, or activated; what is slack, because complete and finished, is dead.

2 The original French achieves a parallel through assonance: "aussi inusable qu'inutilisable."

3 2 Corinthians 4:17.

4 1 Corinthians 15:32.

5 Another parallel through assonance: *couler, se coucher.*

6 John 1:38. Author's brackets.

7 *Dévisagement* derives from *dévisager*, to look at

intently. Both words, of course, contain the noun *visage*, face, which will figure later in the author's reference to Levinas.

III An event is possible

1 From *eventual* in the sense of "relating to events," rather than of "happening in good time."

2 1 Corinthians 15:45, King James translation. The author speaks of the "old" and the "new" Adam.

3 Again, in the sense of "relating to events."

4 These quotations, and several occurring below, are translated directly from the renderings in the original French of this book, with inspiration from the relevant verses of the King James Bible.

5 Author's brackets.

6 *Matriciel* (from *matrix*), of the womb. In this context, fundamental and generative.

7 Here the King James.

8 John 2:1.

9 John 10:19.

10 John 13:19. In the King James: ". . . that I am he."

11 John 8:58.

12 John 1:26. Author's brackets.

13 John 9:26–7.

14 John 1:4. In the King James: "In him was life."

15 Ibid.

IV What is it to be alive?

1 John 5:26, to be exact.
2 John 5:21. Author's brackets, although his parenthesis reads: "font [rendent] vivant."
3 John 5:40.
4 Author's brackets.
5 John 12:25.
6 Author's brackets.
7 1 Corinthians 15:44. The King James substitutes *natural* for Jullien's *psychique*.
8 In the sense of wellspring.
9 "Shall be" in the King James.
10 John 4:7–14. Author's brackets.
11 John 4:31–8.
12 Translator's parenthesis. The French word *esprit* can mean spirit, mind, or wit.
13 The French text provides the assonant pair "s'évase et s'évade."

V The logic of de-coincidence

1 John 12:25. Author's brackets.
2 John 14:3.
3 Another assonant pair in the original French: *regard* (look, or perspective) and *égard* (regard in the sense of respect).
4 3:19.
5 I.e., shift her away from her normal conception of things, not drive her crazy.
6 Verses 26–59.

7 Verses 1–21.
8 Stated in the Bible in the first person: "lay down my life that I might take it again."
9 Verse 60.
10 Verse 43.
11 Verse 8.
12 Confucius, *The Analects of Confucius*, trans. Arthur Waley, Book XVII, 19, London: George Allen & Unwin, 1938.
13 John 10:8.

VI Reconfiguration of truth

1 Verse 35.
2 Verse 12.
3 Verse 7.
4 Verses 14–18.
5 The King James, in seeming agreement with the author, reads: "What is truth?" The Jerusalem Bible reads: "'Truth?' said Pilate. 'What is that?'"
6 In the King James, the question "Art thou the Christ?" never appears. Instead the priests and Levites ask, "Who art thou?" and John the Baptist confesses, "I am not the Christ."
7 Matthew 27:46, Mark 15:34.
8 Plato, *Theaetetus*, trans. Benjamin Jowett, p. 152.
9 *Croire à* translates more literally to *believe* as a transitive verb, with direct object to follow, but *believe that*, at least in English, makes the author's point more cleanly, or so the translator hopes.

10 English usage here is not as cut and dried as French usage. Anglophones do speak of belief *in* Santa Claus.

11 Heraclitus, *The Fragments of the Work of Heraclitus of Ephesus on Nature*, trans. G. T. W. Patrick, Baltimore: N. Murray, 1889, Fragment I.

12 Verses 31–8.

VII Ex-istence: to dwell in the Other by abiding outside of the world

1 "Eyes of your understanding" in the King James (Ephesians 1:18).

2 Plato, *Phaedrus*, trans. Benjamin Jowett.

3 John 8:7.

4 John 7:7.

5 John 8:23.

6 John 16:33.

7 John 8:23.

8 John 16:28.

9 John 18:20.

10 John 3:16.

11 "My kingdom" in the King James (John 18:36).

12 Verse 16.

13 John 14:20.

14 "By the father" in the King James.

15 Verse 57.

16 "Walk in love" in the King James: Ephesians 5:2.

17 13:4–5.

18 Author's brackets.

19 "Thou knowest that I love thee" in the King James.